Imperium Unseens

Julian Morgan

Copyright © 2014 Julian Morgan
All rights reserved.
ISBN: 1493729799
ISBN-13: 978-1493729791

Edition 1.0.6

All photographs used in this book were taken
by the Author, with the sanction
of the institutions involved.

Any errors and omissions in this book are
the fault of the Author. They will be rectified
as soon as he becomes aware of them.

DEDICATION

For the cohorts who endured:

James, Markus, Sophia

Joshua, Benyamin, Charlotte-Emma, Emelie, Franziska, Laura

Alexandre, Gabriel, Hans-Peter, Leonie

Julia, Karl, Oleg

CONTENTS

Part 1	Introduction to Saucy Unseens	1
	Saucy Unseens	2
Part 2	Introduction to Virgil Unseens	32
	Virgil Unseens	41
Part 3	Introduction to Cicero Unseens	65
	Cicero Unseens	66
Also Available		92
About the Author		94

PREFACE

I began to create this material for students at the European School of Karlsruhe, to help in their preparation for the European Baccalaureate. The priority was to find passages which were entertaining as well as linguistically appropriate. I remember all too well having to slog through turgid, incomprehensible stuff in my time at school and I don't like to inflict this on my students today.

I assembled the first section of this book by scouring through Suetonius and the Historia Augusta. These passages comprised the infamous *Saucy Unseens*, which have served to titillate and torture students in my classroom in recent years. We should be aware that not all of Roman history is true and not all of these events actually happened. But it's kind of fun to read about Caligula's incest and Nero's appalling goings on from the security of a two thousand year gap.

The second section uses passages chosen from the first six books of Virgil's Aeneid. As students do battle with these, it will be a good idea for them to read the books in translation as preparation, so that the main details of the epic story are known and understood. In this way, a lack of context should not be able to block access to the meanings of the passages.

The third section uses extracts chosen from various writings of, or about, Cicero. They represent different areas of the author's output, including philosophical writings and political speeches. Cicero is a difficult writer to translate and many of us grew up hating him because of the sheer density and complexity of his expression. However, when a student can find a way to unlock and understand his meaning, he often provides a satisfying experience in the end.

In writing this book, I wanted to create not just a set of unseens, but a complete toolbox in how to deal with them purposefully. Various online support materials for students or teachers can be downloaded from the website, at www.imperiumlatin.com, which include the Imperium Unseens App, audio files, solutions and mark schemes.

Students who translate unseens often find the process frustrating and annoying and it can be hard to stop the rot when it takes hold. In my experience, those who do best are those who spend the longest time thinking and the shortest time writing. Some advice is given about translation technique on the following pages. These guidelines can be hard to adhere to but they can also lead to spectacular improvements.

ACKNOWLEDGEMENTS

The first version of the Imperium Latin course was developed for use in the European School of Karlsruhe in Germany. Students here played an essential role, contributing practical help and advice in the construction of the original course and extension materials. I am most grateful to them and to those others whose Ideas have fed into this project, who have not had to endure the pains of being in my classroom.

This is a living reference book, which can still be corrected and added to by others: this is something which digital publishing allows very easily. I very much hope that as students and teachers think of ways to improve Imperium Latin Unseens, they will not hold back from making contact with me, so that the materials will continue to evolve through the years.

Thanks go to: Jürgen Springer

GUIDELINES for STUDENTS

If you get the process of doing unseens right, you increase your chances of success dramatically. Here are some tips.

TRUST YOUR OWN MEMORY!

Two don'ts

- ✗ It should only take a few minutes (perhaps 5) to write up a translation, if you know what you are going to write before you start. So don't feel the need to pick up a pen and start writing stuff down until you have spent around 30 minutes thinking.

- ✗ Similarly, don't scrawl garbage all over the unseen, while you are thinking about it. It makes it harder to read - and quite probably, a lot of what you write will be wrong in any case: that's why you wrote it in the first place, because you were desperate.

Ten do's

- ✔ Read the whole passage through from top to bottom, without expecting to understand anything.

- ✔ Read all the bits of English dotted around the unseen which may help, e.g. introduction, stuff on any names, notes, etc. In addition, make sure you use all the material you will find under the header *quibuscum in fauces*: it was included for you for a reason.

- ✔ Read the passage through again, top to bottom, looking for easy bits. There are always some easy bits in any piece of Latin.

- ✔ Read the passage again, top to bottom, looking for hard bits. Do they make any sense at all?

- ✔ In sentences where you need more analysis, consider underlining/highlighting the main verbs. These should be the ones which are indicative. Consider analysing them for person, tense, mood, voice: this may help.

- ✔ Find external subjects for your verbs, if they exist. These should be nouns or pronouns in the nominative case. Remember, singular subjects have singular verbs, plural ones have plurals. This is called concord. If there are no external subjects for the verbs, look at the endings and work out what the (internalised) subjects are, e.g. *audis = you hear*.

- ✔ Match up any adjectives to nouns or pronouns. In many cases the endings will be the same, but not if a 2-1-2 adjective agrees with a 3rd declension noun.

- ✔ Keep returning to the beginning of the unseen and starting again. Every time you get stuck, start again at the beginning. This technique works!

- ✔ If your interpretation is nonsense, then it's wrong. It wasn't nonsense when it was written, so you can be sure you are missing something. If all else fails, you will have to make an intelligent guess.

- ✔ Try not to start writing before the whole thing makes sense. If you run out of time, fine, start writing earlier, but see **don't note 1** above.

Putting the pieces together

Part 1 Introduction to Saucy Unseens

This material was assembled after a careful sifting through of the evidence. I have dug in the dirt and chosen passages which could shock as well as entertain.

Suetonius wrote the Lives of the Caesars, which is how he referred to the emperors. He was a gossipy old so-and-so, who tried to track down all the nasty things he could find in his research and always tried to say something scurrilous if he could, even about those emperors whose habits seemed vaguely normal. It should be remembered that he was basically in the pay of the emperor Hadrian, and his task was to write biographies of all his imperial predecessors. The aim was to make them look as bad as possible, so that Hadrian would exude positive vibes to the contemporary readership, reminding them of the glory days of Augustus and of how things had degenerated steadily since then. Suetonius was in fact so irritating that he once even managed to get himself kicked out of Britain by his boss, for being too familiar with his wife.

Given that Suetonius lived under Hadrian, it should be obvious that the emperors after him (well, actually, including him) would be written about by others. The Historia Augusta is the natural follow-up to the Lives of the Caesars, though its date and its authorship are both mired in doubt. It is likely to have been the work of more than one hand, though we shall probably never know to whom any of those hands belonged. Suffice to say that the tone of Suetonius is echoed regularly throughout.

In all of these unseens, students should note that most verbs with no external subjects have as their subjects the particular emperor in the title. So in the life of Titus, if it says *petivit* and there is no external subject, it means *he sought*, where *he* is usually going to mean *Titus*. This might be a case of stating the flaming obvious, but nonetheless, it is something which even good students can find bewildering at the beginning.

When it comes to veracity, it is impossible to know how much of this material is true. My own preference is to suspend reality a bit, and simply to enjoy what Suetonius and the other authors wrote. Certainly, there is some truth in these passages, but how much and where is a huge area of study, which need not detain Latin language students unnecessarily. The main thing is to enjoy the salacious nonsense which follows, though students should ask themselves about the probability of the events being true, rather than accepting them as fact.

1. Suetonius describes how Julius Caesar had affairs with the wives of various famous Romans. His favourite by far was Servilia, the mother of Brutus, to whom he gave all sorts of gifts, including an especially valuable pearl.

(Life of Julius Caesar, 50, with omissions)

pronum et **sumptuosum** in libidines fuisse **constans** opinio est, plurimasque et illustres feminas **corrupisse**, in quibus Postumiam Servi Sulpici, Lolliam Auli Gabini, Tertullam Marci Crassi, etiam **Cn.** Pompei Muciam.

sed ante alias **dilexit** Marci Bruti matrem Serviliam, cui et primo suo consulatu **sexagiens sestertium margaritam mercatus est** et bello civili super alias donationes amplissima praedia ex auctionibus **hastae** minimo **addixit**.

quibuscum in fauces

pronus, prona, pronum	inclined towards
sumptuosus, sumptuosa, sumptuosum	extravagant
constans, constans, constans	fixed
corrumpo, corrumpere, corrupi, corruptum	I corrupt, seduce
Cn.	Cnaeus
diligo, diligere, dilexi, dilectum	I love
sexagiens sestertium	worth six million sesterces
margarita, margaritae, f	pearl
mercor, mercari, mercatus sum	I buy
hasta, hastae, f	a spear (set up to mark an auction taking place)
addico, addicere, addixi, addictum	I make over to, award

2. Suetonius describes how the Emperor Augustus committed adultery on several occasions, including with his then wife-to-be Livia. His former wife Scribonia had objected to his mistress and her influence on him.

(Life of Augustus, 69)

adulteria quidem exercuisse **ne** amici **quidem** negant, excusantes sane non **libidine**, sed **ratione** commissa, quo facilius consilia adversariorum per cuiusque mulieres exquireret. Marcus Antonius super festinatas Liviae nuptias **obiecit** et feminam **consularem** e triclinio viri **coram** in cubiculum abductam, rursus in convivium rubentibus **auriculis incomptiore** capillo reductam; dimissam Scriboniam, quia liberius **doluisset** nimiam potentiam **paelicis**.

quibuscum in fauces

ne... quidem	not even
libido, libidinis, f	lust
ratio, rationis, f	policy
obicio, obicere, obieci, obiectum	I object
consularis, consularis, consulare	of an ex-consul
coram	openly
auricula, auriculae, f	ear
incomptus, incompta, incomptum	unkempt, dishevelled
doleo, dolere, dolui, dolitum	I complain about
paelex, paelicis, f	mistress

3. *Suetonius describes how the emperor Tiberius became a peeping Tom on the island of Capri, during his retirement. Although an old man, he made himself sexually excited by watching others make love and by collecting dirty pictures, statues and books.*

(Life of Tiberius, 43)

secessu vero Caprensi etiam **sellaria** excogitavit, sedem **arcanarum** libidinum, in quam undique conquisiti puellarum et **exoletorum** greges monstrosique **concubitus repertores**, quos **spintrias** appellabat, triplici serie conexi, in vicem **incestarent** coram ipso, ut aspectu deficientis libidines excitaret. cubicula **plurifariam** disposita **tabellis** ac **sigillis** lascivissimarum picturarum et figurarum adornavit librisque **Elephantidis instruxit**, ne cui in opera edenda exemplar deesset.

quibuscum in fauces

secessus, secessus, m	retirement
sellarium, sellarii, n	small room
arcanus, arcana, arcanum	secret
exoletus, exoleti, m	male prostitute
concubitus, concubitus, m	sexual intercourse
repertor, repertoris, m	expert
spintria, spintriae, m	toy-boy
incesto, incestare, incestavi, incestatum	I pollute, defile
plurifariam	in many places
tabella, tabellae, f	picture
sigillum, sigilli, n	relief carving
Elephantis, Elephantidis, f	Elephantis, a place in Egypt famous for its rude books
instruo, instruere, instruxi, instructum	I furnish

4. Suetonius describes how Caligula came to power by seducing the wife of the ambitious Praetorian Guard commander Macro, and then killing the emperor Tiberius with his own bare hands.

(Life of Caligula, 12, with omissions)

Naeviam, Macronis uxorem, qui tum praetorianis cohortibus praeerat, **sollicitavit** ad **stuprum**, pollicitus et matrimonium suum, si potitus imperio fuisset. per hanc **insinuatus** Macroni veneno Tiberium aggressus est, spirantique adhuc detrahi anulum et **pulvinum** iussit inici atque etiam **fauces** manu sua **oppressit**, liberto, qui ob atrocitatem **facinoris** exclamaverat, confestim in **crucem** acto.

quibuscum in fauces

sollicito, sollicitare, sollicitavi, sollicitatum	I lure
stuprum, stupri, n	seduction
insinuo, insinuare, insinuavi, insinuatum	I introduce to
pulvinus, pulvini, n	cushion, pillow
fauces, faucium, f pl	jaws
opprimo, opprimere, oppressi, oppressum	I crush
facinus, facinoris, n	deed, crime
crux, crucis, f	cross, crucifixion

5. *Suetonius describes how the emperor Caligula had sexual relationships with each of his three sisters. His favourite was Drusilla, with whom he had sexual experiences at a very young age, and for whom he retained a special love later on in life.*

(Life of Caligula, 24, slightly adapted)

cum omnibus sororibus suis consuetudinem **stupri** fecit plenoque **convivio** singulas infra se vicissim conlocabat uxore supra cubante. ex iis Drusillam **vitiavisse** virginem **praetextatus** adhuc creditur atque etiam in **concubitu** eius quondam deprehensus est ab Antonia **avia**, apud quam simul **educabantur**; mox Lucio Cassio Longino consulari **conlocatam** abduxit et in modum iustae uxoris **propalam** habuit; heredem quoque bonorum atque imperii aeger eam instituit. eadem defuncta **iustitium** indixit.

quibuscum in fauces

stuprum, stupri, n   seduction, defilement
convivium, convivii, n   dinner party
vitio, vitiare, vitiavi, vitiatum   I seduce, defile
praetextatus, praetextata, praetextatum   wearing a boy's toga
(it means he'd be less than 17 years old)

concubitus, concubitus, m   sexual intercourse
avia, aviae, f   grandmother
educo, educare, educavi, educatum   I bring up
conlocatus, conlocata, conlocatum   given in marriage, betrothed
propalam   openly
iustitium, iustitii, n   public holiday

6. Suetonius describes the emperor Caligula's unexpected fascination with Caesonia, a rather plain-looking, older woman who had been married before and had already had children from this relationship.

(Life of Caligula, 25)

Caesoniam neque facie **insigni** neque **aetate integra** matremque iam ex alio viro trium filiarum, sed luxuriae ac **lasciviae** perditae, et ardentius et constantius amavit, ut saepe **chlamyde peltaque** et galea ornatam ac iuxta **adequitantem** militibus ostenderit, amicis vero etiam nudam. uxorio nomine non prius **dignatus est** quam **enixam**, uno atque eodem die professus et maritum se eius et patrem infantis ex ea natae.

quibuscum in fauces

insignis, insignis, insigne	*beautiful*
aetas, aetatis, f	*age*
integer, integra, integrum	*young*
lascivia, lasciviae, f	*perversion*
chlamys, chlamydis, f	*cloak*
pelta, peltae, f	*shield*
adequito, adequitare, adequitavi, adequitatum	*I ride alongside*
dignor, dignari, dignatus sum	*I dignify*
enitor, eniti, enixus sum	*I give birth*

7. Suetonius describes how the emperor Caligula once made a joke about cutting the throats of the two consuls in Rome and how he used to threaten his mistresses before kissing them.

(Life of Caligula, 32-33)

lautiore convivio **effusus** subito in cachinnos consulibus, qui iuxta cubabant, quidnam rideret **blande** quaerentibus: "quid," inquit, "nisi uno meo **nutu** iugulari utrumque vestrum statim posse?"

quotiens uxoris vel amiculae **collum** exoscularetur, addebat: "tam bona cervix simul ac iussero **demetur**." quin et subinde **iactabat exquisiturum** se vel **fidiculis** de Caesonia sua, cur eam tantopere **diligeret**.

quibuscum in fauces

lautus, lauta, lautum	fine
effusus, effusa, effusum	breaking out
blande	politely
nutus, nutus, m	nod of the head
collum, colli, n	neck
demo, demere, dempsi, demptum	I cut off
iacto, iactare, iactavi, iactatum	I boast
exquiro, exquirere, exquisivi, exquisitum	I discover
fiducula, fiduculae, f	instrument of torture
diligo, diligere, dilexi, dilectum	I love

8. Suetonius describes the appearance of the emperor Caligula: he worried that he looked like a goat, so he made it an offence for people to mention them in his presence or to look down on the top of his head. He also used to pull horrible faces in front of a mirror.

(Life of Caligula, 50)

statura fuit **eminenti**, colore expallido, corpore **enormi**, **gracilitate** maxima cervicis et crurum, oculis et temporibus concavis, **fronte** lata et **torva**, capillo raro at circa **verticem** nullo, **hirsutus** cetera. quare transeunte eo prospicere ex superiore parte aut omnino quacumque de causa capram nominare, criminosum et **exitiale** habebatur. vultum vero natura horridum ac **taetrum** etiam ex industria **efferabat** componens ad speculum in omnem terrorem ac formidinem.

quibuscum in fauces

eminens, eminens, eminens	tall
enormis, enormis, enorme	badly-shaped
gracilitas, gracilitatis, f	thinness
frons, frontis, f	forehead
torvus, torva, torvum	grim
vertex, verticis, m	top of the head
hirsutus, hirsuta, hirsutum	hairy
exitialis, exitialis, exitiale	punishable by death
taeter, taetra, taetrum	foul
effero, efferare, efferavi, efferatum	I make wild

9. *Suetonius describes how Claudius' marriage to Messalina failed. After this, he secretly persuaded the Senate to allow him to marry his niece Agrippina.*

(Life of Claudius 26)

post has Valeriam Messalinam in matrimonium accepit. quam cum **comperisset** super cetera flagitia atque **dedecora** C. Silio etiam nupsisse **dote** inter **auspices** consignata, **supplicio** adfecit confirmavitque permansurum se in **caelibatu** verum **inlecebris** Agrippinae, Germanici fratris sui filiae, per **ius** osculi et blanditiarum occasiones **pellectus** in amorem, **subornavit** proximo senatu qui censerent, cogendum se ad ducendum eam uxorem, quasi reipublicae maxime interesset, dandamque ceteris veniam talium coniugiorum, quae ad id tempus incesta habebantur.

quibuscum in fauces

comperio, comperire, comperi, compertum	I learn
dedecus, dedecoris, n	disgraceful behaviour
dos, dotis, f	dowry, bridal contract
auspex, auspicis, m	witness
supplicium, supplicii, n	death penalty
caelibatus, caelibatus, m	celibacy, single life
inlecebra, inlecebrae, f	attraction
ius, iuris, n	right, privilege
pellego, pellegere, pellegi, pellectum	I seduce
suborno, subornare, subornavi, subornatum	I instruct secretly

10. Suetonius describes how greedy the emperor Claudius was. He always ate and drank too much, and had to be helped to be sick when he was sleeping off the ill effects of his over-indulgence. He often fell asleep during the day, as he slept badly by night.

(Life of Claudius, 33)

nec **temere** umquam triclinio abscessit nisi distentus ac **madens**, et ut statim supino ac per somnum hianti **pinna** in **os** inderetur ad exonerandum stomachum. somni brevissimi erat. nam ante mediam noctem plerumque vigilabat, ut tamen interdiu nonnumquam in iure dicendo obdormisceret vixque ab advocatis **de industria** vocem augentibus excitaretur. libidinis in feminas profusissimae, **marum** omnino **expers**.

quibuscum in fauces

temere — quickly
madens, madens, madens — soaked, i.e. very drunk
pinna, pinnae, f — feather
os, oris, n — mouth
de industria — deliberately
mas, maris, m — man
expers, expers, expers — inexperienced

11. Suetonius describes how the emperor Claudius could be terribly absent-minded. Sometimes, his senior moments made him so bewildered that he forgot where he was, or what he was doing, and he often made stupid comments at the wrong times.

(Life of Claudius, 40)

sermonis vero rerumque tantam saepe neglegentiam ostendit, ut nec quis nec inter quos, quove tempore ac loco verba faceret, scire aut cogitare **existimaretur**. cum de **laniis** ac **vinariis** ageretur, exclamavit in **Curia**, "rogo vos, quis potest sine **offula** vivere?" descripsitque **abundantiam** veterum tabernarum, unde solitus esset vinum olim et ipse petere. de **quaesturae** quodam candidato inter causas **suffragationis** suae posuit, quod pater eius frigidam aquam sibi dedisset.

quibuscum in fauces

sermo, sermonis, m	conversation
existimo, existimare, existimavi, existimatum	I think
lanius, lanii, m	butcher
vinarius, vinarii, m	wine merchant
Curia, Curiae, f	senate house
offula, offulae, f	a little bit, something to chew
abundantia, abundantiae, f	long list
quaestura, quaesturae, f	quaestorship
suffragatio, suffragationis, f	support in an election

12. *Suetonius describes how Claudius died. It is not certain whether it was his foodtaster Halotus who gave him the poisoned mushroom, or his wife Agrippina.*

(Life of Claudius, 44)

et veneno quidem occisum **convenit**; ubi autem et per quem dato, **discrepat**. quidam tradunt **epulanti** in arce cum sacerdotibus per Halotum **spadonem praegustatorem**; alii domestico convivio per ipsam Agrippinam, quae **boletum** medicatum avidissimo ciborum talium obtulerat. etiam de **subsequentibus** diversa fama est. multi statim hausto veneno obmutuisse aiunt excruciatumque doloribus nocte tota **defecisse** prope lucem.

quibuscum in fauces

convenit	it is agreed
discrepat	there is disagreement
epulor, epulari, epulatus sum	I dine
spado, spadonis, m	eunuch (castrated male)
praegustator, praegustatoris, m	foodtaster
boletus, boleti, m	mushroom
subsequor, subsequi, subsecutus sum	I happen soon afterwards
deficio, deficere, defeci, defectum	I grow weak, die

13. Suetonius describes how the emperor Nero had a boy called Sporus castrated and then took him around with him as his partner, wherever he went. Then, when he had thoughts of committing incest with his mother, a suitable substitute was found.

(Life of Nero, 28)

puerum Sporum exsectis testibus etiam in muliebrem naturam transfigurare conatus cum **dote** et **flammeo** per sollemnia nuptiarum celeberrimo officio deductum ad se **pro** uxore habuit; hunc Sporum, **Augustarum** ornamentis **excultum** lecticaque vectum, et circa conventus mercatusque Graeciae ac mox Romae circa **Sigillaria** comitatus est identidem exosculans.

nam matris concubitum appetisse et ab **obtrectatoribus** eius, ne ferox atque **impotens** mulier et hoc genere gratiae praevaleret, deterritum nemo dubitavit, **utique** postquam **meretricem**, quam fama erat Agrippinae simillimam, inter **concubinas** recepit.

quibuscum in fauces

dos, dotis, f	dowry
flammeum, flammei, n	marriage veil
pro + ablative	instead of
Augusta, Augustae, f	empress
excolo, excolere, excolui, excultum	I dress up
Sigillaria, Sigillariorum, n pl	the Sigillaria (a festival held in honour of Saturn)
obtractor, obtractoris, m	critic
impotens, impotens, impotens	wild, unrestrained
utique = utque	
meretrix, meretricis, f	prostitute
concubina, concubinae, f	mistress

14. Suetonius describes how the emperor Nero became jealous of his step-brother Britannicus for his singing ability and then enlisted the help of the poisoner Locusta to kill him.

(Life of Nero, 33)

Britannicum non minus **aemulatione** vocis, quae illi iucundior **suppetebat**, quam metu ne **quandoque** apud hominum gratiam paterna memoria praevaleret, veneno adgressus est. quod acceptum a quadam Locusta, **venenariorum indice**, cum opinione tardius **cederet** ventre **modo** Britannici **moto**, **accersitam** mulierem sua manu verberavit arguens **pro** veneno remedium dedisse, excusantique minus datum ad occultandam facinoris **invidiam**.

quibuscum in fauces

aemulatio, aemulationis, f	jealousy
suppeto, suppetere, suppetivi, suppetitum	I am
quandoque	at some future point in time
venenarius, venenaria, venenarium	to do with poison
index, indicis, m	expert
cedo, cedere, cessi, cessum	I take effect
modo	only
moveo, movere, movi, motum	I am upset
accerso, accersere, accersivi, accersitum	I send for, summon
pro + ablative	instead of
invidia, invidiae, f	evil intention

15. *Suetonius describes how greedy Galba was. He had huge meals served up and then passed on the leftovers to his attendants. He preferred male lovers and when he first heard about Nero's death, he felt an immediate desire to make love to an old flame, called Icelus.*

(Life of Galba, 22)

cibi plurimi **traditur**, quem tempore hiberno etiam ante lucem capere **consuerat**, inter cenam vero usque eo abundantis, ut **congestas** super manus **reliquias** circumferri iuberet spargique ad pedes stantibus. libidinis in **mares** pronior et eos non nisi **praeduros exoletosque**: **ferebant** in Hispania Icelum e veteribus concubinis de Neronis exitu nuntiantem non modo artissimis osculis palam exceptum ab eo, sed ut sine mora **velleretur** oratum atque seductum.

quibuscum in fauces

trado, tradere, tradidi, traditum	I say
consuerat = consueverat	
congero, congerere, congesti, congestum	I pile up
reliquiae, reliquiarum, f pl	leftovers
mas, maris, m	man
praedurus, praedura, praedurum	very strong
exoletus, exoleti, m	male prostitute
fero, ferre, tuli, latum	I say
vello, vellere, vulsi, vulsum	I make love to

16. *Suetonius describes how Nero's friend Otho helped out while the Emperor was plotting to kill his mother. Later, he looked after Nero's girlfriend Poppaea Sabina by taking her from her original husband and marrying her. The plan backfired as Otho fell in love with her.*

(Life of Otho, 3, slightly adapted)

omnium autem consiliorum secretorumque **particeps** die, quem necandae matri Nero **destinarat**, ad avertendam suspicionem cenam utrique exquisitissimae **comitatis** dedit; item Poppaeam Sabinam tunc adhuc amicam eius, **abductam** marito **demandatamque** interim sibi, nuptiarum specie recepit, nec corrupisset contentus, adeo **dilexit** ut ne rivalem quidem Neronem **aequo** tulerit **animo**. creditur certe non modo missos ad arcessendam **astantem** miscentemque frustra minas et preces ac **depositum** reposcentem.

quibuscum in fauces

particeps, participis, m	confidant
destinarat = destinaverat	
comitas, comitatis, f	elegance
abduco, abducere, abduxi, abductum	I steal from
demando, demandare, demandavi, demandatum	I hand over
diligo, diligere, dilexi, dilectum	I love
aequo animo	calmly
asto, astare, astiti	I stand waiting
depono, deponere, deposui, depositum	I leave in the care of

17. Suetonius describes how the emperor Vitellius made some extremely tasteless comments when visiting a battlefield and when looking at the gravestone of his predecessor Otho.

(Life of Vitellius, 10, slightly adapted)

utque **campos**, in quibus pugnatum est, adiit, **abhorrentes** quosdam **cadaverum tabem** detestabili voce confirmare ausus est, optime olere occisum hostem et melius civem. nec eo **setius** ad leniendam gravitatem odoris plurimum **meri** propalam hausit passimque divisit. pari vanitate atque insolentia **lapidem memoriae** Othonis inscriptum intuens, dignum eo **Mausoleo** ait, pugionemque, quo is se occiderat misit Marti dedicandum.

quibuscum in fauces

campus, campi, m	field (used here to describe the site of a battle)
abhorreo, abhorrere, abhorrui	I shudder at, am repelled from
cadaver, cadaveris, n	dead body
tabes, tabis, f	stink
setius	less
merum, meri, n	pure wine
lapis memoriae	gravestone
Mausoleum, Mausolei, n	Mausoleum (large building housing a dead body)

18. Suetonius describes how the emperor Vespasian was known for his sense of humour, mentioning a story about how he teased his son Titus. Right up to the end of his life, Vespasian carried on making jokes.

(Life of Vespasian, 23)

maxime tamen **dicacitatem** adfectabat in **deformibus** lucris, ut invidiam aliqua **cavillatione** dilueret transferretque ad **sales**. reprehendenti filio Tito, quod etiam urinae **vectigal commentus esset,** pecuniam ex prima **pensione** admovit ad nares, **sciscitans** num odore offenderetur; et illo negante: "atqui," inquit, "e **lotio** est."

ac ne metu quidem ac periculo mortis extremo abstinuit iocis. prima quoque morbi **accessione**: "vae," inquit, "puto, deus fio."

quibuscum in fauces

dicacitas, dicacitatis, f	wit, humour
deformis, deformis, deforme	loathsome
cavillatio, cavillationis, f	banter, joke
sal, salis, f	witty remark
vectigal, vectigalis, n	tax
comminiscor, comminisci, commentus sum	I dream up
pensio, pensionis, f	collection, payment
sciscitor, sciscitari, sciscitatus sum	I try to find out
lotium, lotii, n	urine
accessio, accessionis, f	approach

19. Suetonius describes how the emperor Titus kept a troupe of male prostitutes and eunuchs (castrated males). However, despite a reputation for extravagance, Titus never really got a bad name and his reputation stayed intact.

(Life of Titus, 7)

praeter saevitiam suspecta in eo etiam luxuria erat, quod ad mediam noctem **comissationem** cum **profusissimo** quoque familiarum extenderet; nec minus libido, propter **exoletorum** et **spadonum** greges propterque insignem reginae **Berenices** amorem, cum etiam nuptias pollicitus **ferebatur**; suspecta rapacitas, deinque propalam alium Neronem et opinabantur et praedicabant. at illi ea fama pro bono cessit conversaque est in maximas laudes, neque vitio ullo reperto et **contra** virtutibus summis.

quibuscum in fauces

commisatio, commisationis, f	*partying*
profusus, profusa, profusum	*excessive*
exoletus, exoleti, m	*male prostitute*
spado, spadonis, m	*eunuch (castrated male)*
Berenice, Berenices, f	*Berenice, a queen from Judea*
fero, ferre, tuli, latum	*I say*
contra	*on the contrary*

20. *Suetonius describes how Domitian would spend his free time mutilating flies by stabbing them. He left his wife Domitia, because she had fallen in love with an actor called Paris, but he was later persuaded to take her back.*

(Life of Domitian, 3)

inter initia **principatus** cotidie secretum sibi horarum sumere solebat, nec quicquam amplius quam **muscas** captare ac stilo **praeacuto configere**; ut cuidam interroganti, essetne quis intus cum Caesare, non absurde responsum sit a Vibio Crispo, ne muscam quidem.

deinde uxorem Domitiam, ex qua in secundo suo consulatu filium tulerat, **duxit**, alteroque anno consalutavit Augustam; eandem, Paridis histrionis amore **deperditam**, repudiavit, intraque breve tempus **impatiens** discidii, quasi **efflagitante** populo, reduxit.

quibuscum in fauces

principatus, principatus, m	*rule, reign*
musca, muscae, f	*fly*
praeacutus, praeacuta, praeacutum	*very sharp*
configo, configere, confixi, confixum	*I stab*
duco, ducere, duxi, ductum	*I take (as a wife)*
deperdo, deperdere, deperdidi, deperditum	*I lose*
impatiens, impatiens, impatiens	*not able to bear*
efflagito, efflagitare, efflagitavi, efflagitatum	*I demand urgently*

21. The emperor Domitian, though married to Domitia, was indecently attracted to the daughter of his brother Titus. She became pregnant from this association. Eventually, when he forced her to have an abortion, she lost her life.

(Life of Domitian, 22, slightly adapted)

libidinem ingentissimam ac crudelissimam exhibebat; eratque fama, quasi **concubinas** ipse ad Palatium convocaret **nataretque** inter vulgatissimas **meretrices**. fratris filiam, adhuc virginem oblatam in matrimonium sibi cum **devictus** Domitiae nuptiis pertinacissime recusavisset, non multo post alio **conlocatam**, corrupit ultro et quidem vivo etiam tum Tito, mox eam patre ac viro **orbatam** ardentissime palamque dilexit, ut etiam causa mortis **exstiterit** coactae conceptum a se abigere.

quibuscum in fauces

libido, libidinis, f	lust
concubina, concubinae, f	mistress
nato, natare, natavi, natatum	I swim
meretrix, meretricis, f	prostitute
devincio, devincire, devinxi, devictum	I bind together, unite
conloco, conlocare, conlocavi, conlocatum	I betroth
orbo, orbare, orbavi, orbatum	I deprive of, make an orphan
exsisto, exsistere, exstiti	I arise, come about

22. In the Historia Augusta, the writer describes how Hadrian reacted to the loss of his lover Antinous. There were various opinions about the cause of his death, none of which could be proved.

(Life of Hadrian 14)

Antinoum suum, dum per Nilum navigat, perdidit, quem muliebriter **flevit**. de quo **varia** fama est aliis eum **devotum** pro Hadriano **adserentibus**, aliis, quod et forma eius **ostentat** et nimia **voluptas** Hadriani. et Graeci quidem volente Hadriano eum **consecraverunt** oracula per eum dari adserentes, quae Hadrianus ipse conposuisse **iactatur**. fuit enim poematum et litterarum nimium studiosissimus. in voluptatibus nimius. nam et de suis **dilectis** multa versibus composuit.

quibuscum in fauces

fleo, flere, flevi, fletum	I mourn
varius, varia, varium	inconsistent, changing
devoveo, devovere, devovi, devotum	I sacrifice
adsero, adserere, adserui, adsertum	I assert, claim
ostento, ostentare, ostentavi, ostentatum	I make obvious
voluptas, voluptatis, f	sexual urge
consecro, consecrare, consecravi, consecratum	I deify, make a god
iacto, iactare, iactavi, iactatum	I say
dilectus, dilecti, m	favourite

23. In the Historia Augusta, the writer describes how Aelius Verus made inventive use of flower power, in a specially constructed bed. His behaviour was viewed as unseemly but not threatening.

(Life of Aelius 5)

fertur etiam aliud genus **voluptatis**, quod Verus invenerat. nam lectum eminentibus quattuor **anacliteriis** fecerat **minuto reticulo** undique inclusum eumque **foliis** rosae replebat iacensque cum concubinis liliis se tegebat **unctus** odoribus Persicis. iam illa **frequentantur** a nonnullis, quod et **accubitationes** ac mensas de rosis ac liliis fecerit. quae etsi non decora, non tamen ad **perniciem** publicam **prompta sunt**.

quibuscum in fauces

fero, ferre, tuli, latum	I tell, report
voluptas, voluptatis, f	lust
anacliterium, anacliterii, n	side
minutus, minuta, minutum	fine-meshed
reticulum, reticuli, n	net
folium, folii, n	petal
unguo, unguere, unxi, unctum	I anoint
frequento, frequentare, frequentavi, frequentatum	I repeat
accubitatio, accubitationis, f	couch
pernicies, perniciei, f	ruin
promo, promere, prompsi, promptum	I aim at

24. *In the Historia Augusta, the writer describes how Commodus removed all the respectable people who had been assigned to look after him and dedicated himself to a life of pleasure.*

(Life of Commodus 2)

adhibitos custodes vitae suae honestiores ferre non potuit, pessimos quosque **detinuit**. neque umquam **pepercit** vel **pudori** vel sumptui. in domo aleam exercuit. mulierculas formae scitioris ut **prostibula mancipia** perficiens **lupanarium** ad ludibrium pudicitiae **contraxit**. equos **currules** sibi comparavit. aurigae habitu currus **rexit**, gladiatoribus convixit.

quibuscum in fauces

adhibeo, adhibere, adhibui, adhibitum	I assign
detineo, detinere, detinui, detentum	I retain
parco, parcere, peperci, parsum	I spare
pudor, pudoris, m	shameful conduct
prostibulum, prostibuli, n	prostitute
mancipium, mancipii, n	slave
lupanarium, lupanarii, n	brothel
contraho, contrahere, contraxi, contractum	I establish
currulis, currulis, currule	of a chariot
rego, regere, rexi, rectum	I drive

25. In the Historia Augusta, the writer describes some especially unpleasant and tasteless practical jokes carried out by Commodus.

(Life of Commodus 10-11)

adulescens omne genus hominum **infamavit**, quod erat secum, et ab omnibus est infamatus. in iocis quoque perniciosus. habuit et hominem **pene** prominentem ultra **modum** animalium, quem **onon** appellabat, sibi carissimum. quem et **ditavit** et sacerdotio Herculis **rustici** praeposuit.

dicitur saepe pretiosissimis cibis humana **stercora** miscuisse nec abstinuisse **gustum** aliis, ut putabat, inrisis.

quibuscum in fauces

infamo, infamare, infamavi, infamatum	I bring into disrepute
penis, penis, m	penis
modus, modi, m	size
onon	donkey (this is a Greek word in the accusative case)
dito, ditare, ditavi, ditatum	I reward with money
rusticus, rustica, rusticum	of the countryside
stercus, stercoris, n	excrement
gustus, gustus, m	tasting

26. *In the Historia Augusta, the writer describes how Caracalla became the lover and husband of his stepmother Julia, after she seduced him.*

(Life of Caracalla 10)

interest scire **quemadmodum** novercam suam Iuliam uxorem **duxisse** dicatur. quae cum esset pulcherrima et quasi per neglegentiam se maxima corporis parte **nudasset** dixissetque **Antoninus** "vellem, si liceret", respondisse **fertur**: "si libet, licet. **an** nescis te imperatorem esse et leges dare, non accipere?" quo audito nuptias eas celebravit, quas, si sciret se leges dare vere, solus prohibere debuisset. matrem enim (non alio dicenda erat nomine) **duxit** uxorem.

quibuscum in fauces

interest	it is of interest
quemadmodum	how
duco, ducere, duxi, ductum	I take as a wife
nudasset = nudavisset	
Antoninus, Antonini, m	Caracalla
fero, ferre, tuli, latum	I say
an	or (introduces a question)

27. In the Historia Augusta, the writer describes how the emperor punished in a most bizarre fashion two soldiers who had made love to their host's maidservant.

(Life of Macrinus 12)

longum est eius **crudelitates** omnes aperire, at tamen unam ostendam non magnam, ut ipse credebat, sed omnibus tyrannicis immanitatibus **tristiorem**. cum quidam milites ancillam hospitis iam diu **pravi pudoris affectassent** atque per quendam **frumentarium** ille didicisset, adduci eos iussit interrogavitque, utrum esset factum. quod cum **constitisset**, duos boves mirae magnitudinis vivos subito aperiri iussit atque his singulos milites inseri capitibus, ut secum conloqui possent, **exertis**.

quibuscum in fauces

crudelitas, crudelitatis, f	act of cruelty
tristis, tristis, triste	unpleasant
pravus, prava, pravum	bad
pudor, pudoris, m	reputation
affecto, affectare, affectavi, affectatum	I make love to
frumentarius, frumentarii, m	grain seller
constisto, consistere, constiti, consistum	I am established
exero, exerere, exerui, exertum	I stretch out

28. In the Historia Augusta, the writer describes how the emperor's mother Symiamira lived as a prostitute and how his father's identity could not be firmly established. NB – the emperor was known by two names; as Varius, or as Heliogabalus.

(Life of Heliogabalus 2)

hic tantum Symiamirae matri **deditus** fuit, ut sine illius **voluntate** nihil in re publica faceret, cum ipsa **meretricio** more vivens in aula omnia turpia exerceret, **Antonino** autem **Caracallo stupro** cognita, ita ut hic vel Varius vel Heliogabalus **vulgo** conceptus putaretur; et aiunt quidam Varii etiam nomen idcirco eidem **inditum** a condiscipulis, quod vario semine, de meretrice **utpote**, conceptus videretur.

quibuscum in fauces

dedo, dedere, dedidi, deditum	I devote
voluntas, voluntatis, f	approval
meretricius, meretricia, meretricium	of a prostitute
Antonino... Caracallo	Antoninus Caracalla was a previous emperor
stuprum, stupri, n	sexual relationship
vulgo	commonly
indo, indere, indedi, inditum	I give to
utpote	as you might say

29. In the Historia Augusta, the writer describes how the emperor used his agents to bring well-endowed men to him in Rome. He performed the part of Venus in a play about the Judgement of Paris, which became a sex game held on stage.

(Life of Heliogabalus 5)

Romae denique nihil egit aliud, nisi ut **emissarios** haberet, qui ei bene **vasatos** perquirerent eosque ad aulam perducerent, ut eorum conditionibus frui posset. agebat praeterea domi fabulam Paridis ipse Veneris personam **subiens**, ita ut subito vestes ad pedes defluerent, nudusque una manu ad mammam altera **pudendis** adhibita **ingenicularet posterioribus** eminentibus in **subactorem reiectis** et oppositis.

quibuscum in fauces

emissarius, emissarii, m	agent
vasatus, vasati, m	well-endowed male
subeo, subire, subii, subitum	I take over
pudenda, pudendorum, n pl	private parts
ingeniculo, ingeniculare, ingeniculavi, ingeniculatum	I kneel
posteriores, posteriorum, m pl	buttocks
subactor, subactoris, m	second actor
reiectus, reiecta, reiectum	pushed back

30. In the Historia Augusta, the writer describes two of the emperor's strange practices. He used to terrify his friends by sending wild animals into their bedrooms, and found it amusing to watch others feeling rather deflated at the dinner table.

(Life of Heliogabalus 24)

ebrios amicos plerumque **claudebat** et subito nocte leones et leopardos et ursos **exarmatos** immittebat, ita ut **expergefacti** in cubiculo eodem leones, ursos, **pardos** cum luce vel, quod est gravius, nocte invenirent, ex quo plerique **exanimati sunt**. multis **vilioribus** amicis **folles** pro **accubitis** sternebat eosque **reflabat** prandentibus illis, ita ut plerumque subito sub mensis invenirentur prandentes.

quibuscum in fauces

claudo, claudere, clausi, clausum	I lock in
exarmatus, exarmata, exarmatum	with their claws removed
expergefacio, expergefacere, expergefeci, expergefactum	I wake up
pardus, pardi, m	panther
exanimo, exanimare, exanimavi, exanimatum	I scare to death
vilior, vilior, vilius	less important
follis, follis, m	inflatable bag
accubitum, accubiti, n	couch for dining
reflo, reflare, reflavi, reflatum	I let down, deflate

Introduction to Virgil Unseens

The selection of passages which follows has been taken from Books 1 to 6 of the Aeneid. If you are a teacher, you might want to help your students out by telling them which book to read before giving them a particular unseen to work through in class. If you are a student, it would be a great idea to read the first half of the Aeneid before you start to work through these passages. By doing this, you will gain some familiarity with the characters and the storyline, before you are challenged with the unseen translation itself.

The importance of scansion

When you translate Virgil, you will meet all sorts of problems, unless you learn the basic rules of scansion. To some of you students out there, this may seem like one complication too many, but in fact, it's often the only way to be certain that what you are doing is right. And most of the problems are caused by one singular aspect of language: the letter *a* as an ending in the first declension. If that ending wasn't so problematic – and yes, it seems so simple – then you'd be able quite happily to skip reading this section.

But it is, and you shouldn't.

Explaining the problem

When we write out the first declension, we often use the model noun *puella*. This is declined in the singular as:

Nominative	**puella**
Vocative	**puella**
Accusative	*puellam*
Genitive	*puellae*
Dative	*puellae*
Ablative	**puella**

No problems there, you'd say. But you'd be wrong. Sometimes – and indeed, it happens quite often – you need to know whether the word **puella** is in the nominative, vocative or ablative case. In fact, we can be even more specific, because the vocative normally doesn't cause a problem. You will need to know if **puella** is nominative or ablative.

As a nominative, *puella* would be the subject of the verb, or a complement of it. But as an ablative, it would mean *by, with* or *from* the girl, and you'd have to know which was which before you could translate a sentence. To see this more clearly, take this example, from lines 6 to 8 of Aeneid IV:

postera Phoebea lustrabat lampade terras
umentemque **Aurora** polo dimoverat umbram,
cum sic unanimam adloquitur male **sana** sororem:

Questions

Is **postera** nominative or ablative?
Is **Phoebea** nominative or ablative?
Is **Aurora** nominative or ablative?
Is **sana** nominative or ablative?

What difference could any of these things possibly make?

Well, every difference, actually.

So... how do we solve this set of problems – or in other words, how do we know what to do with all these words ending in -*a*?

The answer to the last question lies in scansion.

Read on...

A definition of metrical units

Each line of Virgil's text is written as a line of so-called *dactylic hexameters*. The word *dactylic* comes from the Greek word *daktulos* which means *finger*, because a so-called **dactyl** has one long part and two short parts. We could think of this as a *trumpety*. Here we can see (or hear) that while *trump* sounds quite long, the syllables *e* and *ty* both seem quite short. This can be marked up as *trūmpĕtў*, where the markings above the letters signify that the first syllable is long and the next two syllables are short.

Virgil has two more metrical units up his sleeve, however. The one we call a **spondee** can be thought of as *trump trump*. Both trumps are long, so this could be marked up as *trūmp trūmp*.

And finally, the one we call a **trochee** can be thought of as *trumpet*. While *trump* is long, as we have seen, the *et* is clearly not so long, so this could be marked up as *trūmpĕt*.

To summarise, Virgil used three types of metrical unit in his writing, called **dactyls**, **spondees** and **trochees**. The possible ways of arranging these metrical units were limited by the genre in which Virgil was writing, which imposes that each line must have six *metra* (measures) dominated by the *dactyl*. So Virgil had to split each line into 6 divisions, which we now call *feet*. The fifth foot (this is important) is always *trūmpĕtў* (a *dactyl*), whereas anything in the first four feet can be either *trūmpĕtў* (a *dactyl*), or *trūmp trūmp* (a *spondee*). The sixth foot is normally *trūmp trūmp* (a *spondee*) but can also be *trūmpĕt* (a *trochee*).

By the way, for metrical purposes, one complete unit of *ĕtў* is worth one *trūmp*. If this was music, you could call a *trūmp* a crotchet, while an *ĕ* or a *tў* would each be a quaver. If this is all getting too complicated, you could simply say that one long syllable has the same metrical value as two short ones.

In any case, the possible arrangements of feet in a line are:

trūmpĕtў	trūmpĕtў	trūmpĕtў	trūmpĕtў		trūmp trūmp
or	or	or	or	trūmpĕtў	or
trūmp trūmp	trūmp trūmp	trūmp trūmp	trūmp trūmp		trūmpĕt

If you have an aversion to brass instruments, you could strip this down to:

– ⌣ ⌣	– ⌣ ⌣	– ⌣ ⌣	– ⌣ ⌣		– –
or	or	or	or	– ⌣ ⌣	or
– –	– –	– –	– –		– ⌣

Now try this well-known line of English verse:

Down in a deep-dark dell stood an old cow munching a beanstalk.

It can be translated into *trumpety trumps* as:

trūmpĕtў trūmp trūmp   trūmpĕtў trūmp trūmp trūmpĕtў trūmp trūmp

Or you could write it thus:

Dōwn ĭn ă deēp-dārk dēll stoŏd ăn ōld cōw mūnchĭng ă beānstālk.

Notice that when syllable markings are used, they sit above the vowels in the syllables.

Foot markers and Caesuras

In order to see where the *trumpety trump trumps* go, foot markers are used, a bit like bar lines in a piece of music. Have a look now:

Dōwn ĭn ă ⏐deēp-dārk ⏐dēll stoŏd ăn ⏐ōld cōw ⏐mūnchĭng ă ⏐beānstālk.

After this, we should also add in a double vertical line, called a *caesura*, where a reader could take short breath (often this coincides with a punctuation mark). The caesura is normally found in the second, third or fourth foot and it **never** coincides with a foot marker. In the example, this could give us:

Dōwn ĭn ă ⏐deēp-dārk ⏐dēll ‖ stoŏd ăn ⏐ōld cōw ⏐mūnchĭng ă ⏐beānstālk.

Elisions

An *elision* is a particularly horrible invention of the Latin language. It refers to where two words meet and when part of a syllable goes missing. You cannot actually *see* it - but you have to *know* it is happening. When you scan a line of Virgil, you always have to look for these, and sometimes they are quite easy to miss.

Let's try one little parallel first in English, which might help explain the phenomenon. When you say the words, *I am*, you often omit the letter *a,* and you get *I'm*. This is easy, because it is marked by an apostrophe, so you know what has happened. But in order to understand the devious nature of Latin, you have to realise that they didn't use apostrophes here to show where part of a word went missing. In Latin, you'd still see *I am* printed on the page, but you'd never get the line to scan properly unless you removed the syllable created by the second vowel. Even then, this parallel doesn't work, because Latin would actually ignore the *I* syllable and place a scansion mark on the remaining part, which is the *a* of the word *am*. (I warned you this would be horrible.)

Elisions in Latin happen in two situations:

> when the first word ends in a vowel and the next word begins with a vowel, as in *puella ad,* which would be pronounced as *puell' ad*.

> when the first word ends in the letter *m* and the next word begins with a vowel, as in *puellam ad,* which would also be pronounced *puell' ad*.

The problem with the letter *i*

Take great care with the letter *i,* which can be a vowel or a consonant in Latin. For example, in the word *in*, the letter *i* is a vowel, but in the word *iam*, it is a consonant, pronounced like the letter *y* in English. If it is used as a consonant, it cannot ever be part of an elision.

Marking elisions

To mark an elision, you should use a combining symbol, as seen here: puella ͜ ad. Once you have done this, you can mark the syllable *ad* with a long or a short, as appropriate, but you should then ignore the last letter *a* of the word *puella*, as it actually no longer exists in a metrical capacity.

The process of scanning a line of Virgil

> ➤ Always copy the text out first onto a piece of paper and don't wreck a good copy.
> ➤ Make sure your single line is written on one continuous line.
> ➤ Do all your markings with a pencil, so you can erase them when you get them wrong. Trust me, you will.

The first thing you should do is to check for elisions. If you forget to do this first, you may have problems later. After doing this, you should be able to spot *trumpety trump trump* at the end of the line. Mark this in, as seen here:

postera Phoebea lustrabat ⁞ lāmpădĕ ⁞ tērrās
umentemque Aurora polo dim ⁞ ōvĕrăt ⁞ ūmbrām,
cum sic unanimam adloquitur male ⁞ sānă sŏr ⁞ ōrĕm:

Your only potential problem is that every once in a while, Virgil used a trochee in the sixth foot, so you might just occasionally see a *trumpety trumpet,* instead. See line 3 above.

Either way, you should now have the first to fourth feet left to scan, and you need to insert the appropriate markings above all the syllables remaining. If you want, you can count up the number of syllables left. And if there are less than 8, you have screwed up. Likewise, if there are more than 12, you need to start again.

If there are exactly 8, you're in luck. This means the line must be:

trump trump, trump trump, trump trump, trump trump, trumpety, trump trump[*]
[*] *or trumpet*

Similarly, if there are exactly 12, you're also in luck. This means the line must be:

trumpety, trumpety, trumpety, trumpety, trumpety, trump trump[*]
[*] *or trumpet*

If, as is most probably the case, the number of syllables is between 8 and 12, then it's best not to rely on guesswork and you will have to start using some rules. So it's time to learn a few...

Long syllables

Most syllables are long when they are followed by two consonants. These consonants do not have to be in the same word, or words. For example, the following syllables which are marked long in the examples below are all affected by this rule:

pōstera Phoebea **lūs**tra**bāt** | **lāmp**ădĕ | **tērr**ās

Why not the last *a* of postera? I hear you say. Well, the letters *ph* form one very tight sound and could even be represented in our language as the letter *f*. This is because the original word comes from Greek. And unfortunately, the *p* and the *h* together don't necessarily count as two letters in scansion. Sorry about that.

If you know that something is accusative plural, such as puellas, or filios, then the last syllables are usually long.

pōstera Phoebea lūstrabāt | lāmpădĕ | tērr**ās**

If two vowels combine to make one sound (this is called a diphthong) then this is almost always long. Such combinations would include *ae*, *au* or *oe*. See the marking below.

pōstera **Phoē**bea lūstrabāt | lāmpădĕ | tērrās

Short syllables

The suffix -*que* is usually short, unless it is followed by two consonants (see rule above).

If something *looks* short, it probably is, but don't be rushed into guesswork. The letter *a*, for example, can be long or short, which is the main reason these pages were written (see above).

When a first declension noun is in the nominative singular, the last letter *a* is short, but when the same noun is in the ablative singular, it's long. The letter *i* is often short in words where a vowel follows it, such as audĭunt, but this rule can also get you into trouble if you apply it too rigorously.

The problem with the letter *h*

When a word starts with the letter *h*, this is not really considered to be a consonant in Latin, but more like a vowel with a breathing on it. This is how the French pronounce the word *horrible*, and as you will easily understand – the *h* is silent in this word.

Once bitten

If you have read these rules, the best thing will be to get some practice done and see if you can get used to quick and easy scansion, while you are doing your unseen. For the time being, just try to insert all the relevant scansion markings for the following passage, under your own steam. It can be found again on page 55, as one of the unseen passages in this collection.

at regina gravi iamdudum saucia cura
vulnus alit venis et caeco carpitur igni.
multa viri virtus animo multusque recursat
gentis honos; haerent infixi pectore vultus
verbaque nec placidam membris dat cura quietem.
postera Phoebea lustrabat lampade terras
umentemque Aurora polo dimoverat umbram,
cum sic unanimam adloquitur male sana sororem:
"Anna soror, quae me suspensam insomnia terrent!
quis novus hic nostris successit sedibus hospes,
quem sese ore ferens, quam forti pectore et armis!"

Give yourself a chance to succeed first, before you give up and turn the page!

A solution to the problem

āt rēg|īnă ‖ gră|vī iām|dūdūm |saūcĭă |cūrā

vūlnŭs ă|līt vē|nīs ‖ ēt |caēcō |cārpĭtŭr |īgnī.

mūltă vĭ|rī vīr|tūs ănĭ|mō ‖ mūlt|ūquĕ rĕ|cūrsāt

gēntĭs hŏ|nōs; ‖ haēr|ēnt īnf|īxī |pēctŏrĕ |vūltūs

vērbăquĕ |nēc plăcĭ|dām mēm|brīs ‖ dāt |cūră quĭ|ētēm.

pōstĕră |Phoēbē|ā ‖ lūst|rābāt |lāmpădĕ |tērrās

ūmēnt|ēmque ‿Aū|rōră ‖ pŏ|lō dīm|ōvĕrāt |ūmbrām,

cūm sīc |ūnănĭm|am ‿ādlŏquĭt|ūr ‖ mălĕ |sānă sŏr|ōrĕm:

'Ānnă sŏ|rōr, ‖ quaē |mē sūsp|ēnsam ‿īn|sōmnĭă |tērrēnt!

quīs nŏvŭs |hīc ‖ nōst|rīs sūcc|ēssīt |sēdĭbŭs |hōspēs,

quēm sēs|e ‿ōrĕ fĕr|ēns, ‖ quām |fōrtī |pēctŏre ‿ĕt |ārmīs!'

31. *Virgil introduces his story of Aeneas, describing how Juno, queen of Heaven, worked against him on his way to the city of Lavinium in Latium, where he brought his Trojan gods with him. He calls upon his Muse as a source of inspiration, to tell the reasons for Juno's anger.*

(Aeneid I, lines 1-11)

arma virumque cano, Troiae qui primus ab **oris**
Italiam, fato profugus, **Laviniaque** venit
litora, **multum** ille et terris iactatus et alto
vi superum saevae memorem Iunonis ob iram;
multa quoque et bello passus, dum conderet urbem,
inferretque deos Latio, genus **unde** Latinum,
Albanique patres, atque altae moenia Romae.
Musa, mihi causas memora, quo **numine laeso**,
quidve dolens, regina **deum** tot **volvere** casus
insignem pietate virum, tot adire **labores**
impulerit. tantaene animis caelestibus irae?

quibuscum in fauces

ora, orae, f — shore
Lavinius, Lavinia, Lavinium — of Lavinium, a town in Latium
multum — much (adverb)
unde — from where came
numen, numinis, n — divine spirit
laedo, laedere, laesi, laesum — I offend
deum = deorum
volvo, volvere, volvi, volutum — I face
labor, laboris, m — struggle

32. *Aeneas and his men are battered by a storm and eventually come to shore in Libya. The inlet they find is a natural harbour surrounded by woods. It is dark and full of foreboding.*

(Aeneid I, lines 157-165)

defessi Aeneadae, quae proxima litora, cursu
contendunt petere, et Libyae **vertuntur** ad oras.
est in **secessu** longo locus: insula portum
efficit **obiectu** laterum, quibus omnis ab alto
frangitur inque **sinus scindit** sese unda reductos.
hinc atque hinc vastae rupes geminique minantur
in caelum scopuli, quorum sub vertice late
aequora tuta silent; tum silvis **scaena coruscis**
desuper horrentique atrum nemus imminet umbra.

quibuscum in fauces

vertor, verti, versus sum	I turn my course
secessus, secessus, m	seclusion, remote area
obiectus, obiectus, m	projection
sinus, sinus, m	bay
scindo, scindere, scidi, scissum	I cut
scaena, scaenae, f	backcloth
coruscus, corusca, coruscum	shimmering

33. *Venus approaches Jupiter, to ask if he has changed his mind about helping Aeneas, her son. He had promised that the descendants of the Trojans would rule the world, but recent events seem to show that they are facing more difficulties than had been expected.*

(Aeneid I, lines 227-237)

atque illum **talis** iactantem pectore curas
tristior et lacrimis oculos suffusa **nitentis**
adloquitur Venus: "O qui res hominumque deumque
aeternis regis imperiis, et **fulmine** terres,
quid meus Aeneas in te committere **tantum**,
quid Troes **potuere**, quibus, tot funera passis,
cunctus ob Italiam terrarum clauditur **orbis**?
certe hinc Romanos olim, volventibus annis,
hinc fore ductores, revocato a sanguine **Teucri**,
qui mare, qui terras omni **dicione** tenerent,
pollicitus, quae te, **genitor**, sententia vertit?"

quibuscum in fauces

talis = tales
nitentis = nitentes
adloquor, adloqui, adlocutus sum　　　　I address
fulmen, fulminis, n　　　　thunderbolt
tantum　　　　recently
potuere = potuerunt
orbis, orbis, m　　　　ring (orbis terrarum = the world)
Teucer, Teucri, mTeucer　　　　(legendary founder of Troy)
dicio, dicionis, f　　　　control
genitor, genitoris, m　　　　father

34. *Jupiter reassures Venus that the Trojans are fated to be successful, despite the hardships Aeneas is facing now. After 300 years, the city of Rome will be founded by Romulus, and the Romans will eventually build an empire without boundary.*

(Aeneid I, lines 272-283)

hic iam ter centum totos regnabitur annos
gente sub Hectorea, donec regina **sacerdos**,
Marte **gravis**, geminam partu dabit **Ilia** prolem.
inde lupae fulvo nutricis **tegmine** laetus
Romulus **excipiet** gentem, et **Mavortia** condet
moenia, Romanosque suo de nomine dicet.
his ego nec **metas** rerum nec tempora pono;
imperium sine fine dedi. quin aspera Iuno,
quae mare nunc terrasque metu caelumque fatigat,
consilia in melius **referet**, mecumque fovebit
Romanos rerum dominos gentemque togatam:
sic placitum.

quibuscum in fauces

sacerdos, sacerdotis, f	priestess
gravis, gravis, grave	pregnant
Ilia, Iliae, f	Ilia, mother of Romulus
tegmen, tegminis, n	skin
excipio, excipere, excepi, exceptum	I welcome
Mavortius, Mavortia, Mavortium	of Mars
meta, metae, f	boundary
refero, referre, rettuli, relatum	I change

35. *After the murder of Sychaeus by her brother Pygmalion, Dido sees a vision of her husband, who says that she must leave Phoenicia, to make a new settlement in a far-off land. Her tells about some buried treasure which will help to fund her journey.*

(Aeneid I, lines 353-364)

ipsa sed in somnis inhumati venit imago
coniugis, ora modis **attollens** pallida miris,
crudeles aras traiectaque pectora ferro
nudavit, caecumque domus **scelus** omne **retexit**.
tum celerare fugam patriaque excedere suadet,
auxiliumque viae veteres tellure **recludit**
thesauros, ignotum argenti pondus et auri.
his commota fugam Dido sociosque parabat:
conveniunt, quibus aut odium crudele tyranni
aut metus acer erat; **navis**, quae **forte** paratae,
corripiunt, onerantque auro: portantur avari
Pygmalionis **opes** pelago; dux femina facti.

quibuscum in fauces

attollo, attollere	I lift up
nudo, nudare, nudavi, nudatum	I expose
scelus, sceleris, n	crime
retego, retegere, retexi, retectum	I reveal
recludo, recludere, reclusi, reclusum	I reveal
thesaurus, thesauri, m	treasure
navis = naves	
forte	by chance
opes, opum, f pl	wealth

36.   Venus thinks of new ways to make Dido and Aeneas fall in love. She is afraid of Carthage, the double-tongued Tyrians and Juno's anger, so she summons Cupid to help her and appeals to him as her only solution in the crisis.

(Aeneid I, lines 657-666)

at **Cytherea** novas artes, nova pectore versat
consilia, ut faciem mutatus et ora Cupido
pro dulci Ascanio veniat, donisque furentem
incendat reginam, atque ossibus **implicet** ignem;
quippe domum timet **ambiguam** Tyriosque **bilinguis**;
urit atrox Iuno, et sub noctem cura recursat.
ergo his **aligerum** dictis adfatur Amorem:
"nate, meae **vires**, mea magna potentia solus,
nate, patris summi qui tela **Typhoia** temnis,
ad te confugio et supplex tua **numina** posco."

quibuscum in fauces

Cytherea, Cythereae, f	Venus
pro + ablative	in the place of
implico, implicare, implicavi, implicatum	I wind around
ambiguus, ambigua, ambiguum	beset by danger, in danger
bilinguis, bilinguis, bilingue	double-tongued, deceitful
aliger, aligera, aligerum	winged
vires, virum, f pl	strength
temno, temnere, tempsi, temptum	I scorn
Typhoius, Typhoia, Typhoium	aimed at Typhon (a Titan, who was attacked by Jupiter's thunderbolts)
numen, numinis, n	divine power

37. The Trojans decide to grant his life to the Greek captive, Sinon, who claims to have been deceived by his fellow Greeks. King Priam asks him what the purpose was of the Wooden Horse, and Sinon begins his reply with an oath.

(Aeneid II, lines 145-156)

his lacrimis vitam damus et **miserescimus** ultro.
ipse viro primus **manicas** atque **arta** levari
vincla iubet Priamus dictisque ita fatur amicis:
"quisquis es, amissos hinc iam obliviscere Graios
(noster eris) mihique haec **edissere** vera roganti:
quo molem hanc immanis equi statuere? quis auctor?
quidve petunt? quae religio? aut quae machina belli?"
dixerat. ille dolis instructus et arte **Pelasga**
sustulit **exutas** vinclis ad sidera palmas:
"vos, aeterni ignes, et non violabile vestrum
testor numen," ait, "vos arae ensesque nefandi,
quos fugi...

quibuscum in fauces

miseresco, miserescere	*I feel pity*
manica, manicae, f	*manacle, handcuff*
artus, arta, artum	*close-fitting*
edissero, edisserere, edisserui, edissertum	*I tell*
quo	*how*
Pelasgus, Pelasga, Pelasgum	*Greek*
exuo, exuere, exui, exutum	*I strip away, remove*

38. The ghost of the dead Trojan hero Hector appears to Aeneas in his sleep. His appearance is bloody and unkempt, totally unlike when he had been alive fighting against the Greeks.

(Aeneid II, lines 268-279)

tempus erat quo prima **quies** mortalibus **aegris**
incipit et dono divum gratissima serpit.
in somnis, ecce, ante oculos maestissimus Hector
visus adesse mihi largosque effundere **fletus**,
raptatus bigis ut quondam, aterque cruento
pulvere perque pedes traiectus **lora** tumentis.
ei mihi, qualis erat, quantum mutatus ab illo
Hectore qui redit **exuvias** indutus Achilli
vel **Danaum Phrygios iaculatus** puppibus ignis!
squalentem barbam et concretos sanguine crinis
vulneraque illa gerens, quae circum plurima muros
accepit patrios.

quibuscum in fauces

quies, quietis, f	sleep, rest
aeger, aegra, aegrum	weak
fletus, fletus, m	tear, weeping
rapto, raptare, raptavi, raptatum	I drag
bigae, bigarum, f pl	two-horsed chariot
lorum, lori, n	strap
ei	Oh!
exuviae, exuviarum, f pl	spoils
Danaum = Danaorum	
Phrygius, Phrygia, Phrygium	Trojan
iaculor, iaculari, iaculatus sum	I throw

39. Aeneas tells of how he awoke to the sound of Troy's walls being attacked. He climbed on the roof to look out and saw the city being destroyed, which made him think of a cornfield being burned or a river bursting its banks.

(Aeneid II, lines 298-308)

diverso interea **miscentur** moenia luctu,
et magis atque magis, quamquam **secreta** parentis
Anchisae domus arboribusque obtecta **recessit**,
clarescunt sonitus armorumque ingruit horror.
excutior somno et summi **fastigia** tecti
ascensu supero atque **arrectis auribus** asto:
in segetem veluti cum flamma furentibus Austris
incidit, aut rapidus montano flumine **torrens**
sternit agros, **sternit sata** laeta **boumque** labores
praecipitisque trahit silvas; stupet inscius alto
accipiens sonitum saxi de vertice pastor.

quibuscum in fauces

misceo, miscere, miscui, mixtum	I mix up with, embroil
secretus, secreta, secretum	remote
recedo, recedere, recessi, recessum	I stand back
fastigium, fastigii, n	roof (here, plural = singular)
arrigo, arrigere, arregi, arrectum	I concentrate
auris, auris, f	ear, hearing
torrens, torrentis, m	torrent, flood
sterno, sternere, stravi, stratum	I knock down, flatten
sata, satorum, n pl	crops
boumque = bovumque	

40. The son of Achilles, Pyrrhus, slaughters Polites, and then kills his father Priam in a particularly unpleasant and cruel fashion, after the old king tells him that he is an unworthy son of his father.

(Aeneid II, lines 547-558)

cui Pyrrhus: "**referes** ergo haec et nuntius ibis
Pelidae genitori. illi mea tristia facta
degeneremque **Neoptolemum** narrare memento.
nunc morere." hoc dicens altaria ad ipsa trementem
traxit et in multo lapsantem sanguine nati,
implicuitque **comam** laeva, dextraque coruscum
extulit ac lateri **capulo tenus** abdidit ensem.
haec finis Priami fatorum, hic exitus illum
sorte tulit Troiam incensam et prolapsa videntem
Pergama, tot quondam populis terrisque superbum
regnatorem Asiae. iacet ingens litore **truncus**,
avulsumque umeris caput et sine nomine corpus.

quibuscum in fauces

refero, referre, rettuli, relatum	I tell
Pelides, Pelidae, m	Son of Peleus (Achilles)
Neoptolemus, Neoptolemi, m	Neoptolemus – also known as Pyrrhus
coma, comae, f	hair
capulum, capuli, n	hilt (of a sword)
tenus	as far as
sors, sortis, f	lot, destiny
Pergama, Pergamorum, n pl	the Towers of Troy
truncus, trunci, m	trunk of the body

41. After being threatened by Aeneas and his men, the Harpy Celaeno places a curse on them. Jupiter had once foretold this to Phoebus Apollo and he had revealed it to her in turn.

(Aeneid III, lines 250-260)

"accipite ergo animis atque haec mea **figite** dicta,
quae Phoebo pater omnipotens, mihi Phoebus Apollo
praedixit, vobis Furiarum ego maxima **pando**.
Italiam cursu petitis ventisque vocatis:
ibitis Italiam portusque intrare licebit.
sed non **ante** datam **cingetis** moenibus urbem
quam vos dira fames nostraeque iniuria caedis
ambesas subigat malis **absumere** mensas."
dixit, et in silvam pennis ablata refugit.
at sociis subita gelidus formidine sanguis
deriguit.

quibuscum in fauces

figo, figere, fixi, fixum	I fix
pando, pandere, pansi, passum	I reveal
ante... quam	before
cingo, cingere, cinxi, cinctum	I surround
ambedo, ambedere, ambedi, ambesum	I nibble, eat around the edge
absumo, absumere, absumpsi, amsumptum	I eat
derigesco, derigescere, derigui	I freeze, grow stiff

42. When Aeneas and his men arrive in Epirus, they are surprised to see Andromache, the former wife of Hector. She is even more surprised to see them, however, and faints from the shock.

(Aeneid III, lines 306-319)

ut me conspexit venientem et Troïa circum
arma amens vidit, magnis exterrita **monstris**
deriguit visu in medio, calor ossa reliquit;
labitur, et longo **vix** tandem tempore fatur:
"**verane** te facies, verus mihi nuntius adfers,
nate dea? **vivisne**, aut, si lux alma recessit,
Hector ubi est?" dixit, lacrimasque effudit et omnem
implevit clamore locum. vix pauca furenti
subicio, et raris **turbatus** vocibus **hisco**:
"vivo equidem, vitamque extrema per omnia duco;
ne dubita, nam vera vides.
heu, quis te casus deiectam coniuge tanto
excipit, aut quae digna satis fortuna revisit
Hectoris **Andromachen**?"

quibuscum in fauces

monstrum, monstri, n — shocking sight
derigesco, derigescere, derigui — I grow numb, faint
vix — with difficulty
verane = vera – ne
vivisne = vivis – ne
subicio, subicere, subieci, subiectum — I begin to speak
turbo, turbare, turbavi, turbatum — I trouble
hisco, hiscere — I mutter
Andromachen — accusative form of Andromache

43. Aeneas and his men approach Italy for the first time. They are delighted to see the land and raise a shout of joy.

(Aeneid III, lines 521-531)

iamque rubescebat stellis **Aurora fugatis**
cum procul obscuros collis **humilemque** videmus
Italiam. Italiam primus conclamat **Achates**,
Italiam laeto socii clamore salutant.
tum pater Anchises magnum **cratera corona**
induit implevitque mero, divosque vocavit
stans celsa in **puppi**:
"di maris et terrae tempestatumque potentes,
ferte viam vento facilem et **spirate secundi**."
crebrescunt optatae aurae portusque patescit
iam propior, templumque apparet in arce Minervae.

quibuscum in fauces

Aurora, Aurorae, f	Aurora, goddess of the dawn
fugo, fugare, fugavi, fugatum	I put to flight
humilis, humilis, humile	low-lying
Achates, Achatis, m	Achates, a companion of Aeneas
cratera – acc. sing form	mixing bowl
corona, coronae, f	garland
induo, induere, indui, indutum	I decorate
puppis, puppis, f	stern of a ship
spiro, spirare, spiravi, spiratum	I blow
secundus, secunda, secundum	favourable, in the right direction

44. Aeneas and his men meet a Greek left behind by Odysseus, who describes what he has seen in the cave, the home of the Cyclops.

(Aeneid III, lines 618-629)

domus **sanie dapibusque** cruentis,
intus opaca, ingens. ipse **arduus**, altaque pulsat
sidera (di talem terris avertite pestem!)
nec visu facilis nec dictu adfabilis ulli;
visceribus miserorum et sanguine **vescitur** atro.
vidi egomet duo de numero cum corpora nostro
prensa manu magna medio resupinus in antro
frangeret ad saxum, **sanieque** aspersa **natarent
limina**; vidi atro cum membra fluentia **tabo
manderet** et tepidi tremerent sub dentibus artus—
haud impune quidem, nec talia **passus** Ulixes
oblitusve sui est Ithacus discrimine tanto.

quibuscum in fauces

sanies, saniei, f	gore, bloodstain
daps, dapis, f	feast
arduus, ardua, arduum	tall
viscera, viscerum, n pl	entrails, insides
vescor, vesci	I feed on
nato, natare, natavi, natatum	I am flooded
limen, liminis, n	doorway, threshold
tabum, tabi, n	gore, bloody mess
mando, mandere, mandi, mansum	I chew
patior, pati, passus sum	I allow

45. Dido feels love for Aeneas coursing through her veins after seeing him at dinner and hearing him talk about his struggles in Troy. She seeks out her sister, to tell her about her feelings.

(Aeneid IV, lines 1-11)

at regina gravi iamdudum **saucia** cura
vulnus **alit** venis et caeco **carpitur** igni.
multa viri virtus animo multusque recursat
gentis honos; **haerent** infixi pectore **vultus**
verbaque nec placidam membris dat cura quietem.
postera Phoebea lustrabat lampade terras
umentemque **Aurora polo** dimoverat umbram,
cum sic unanimam adloquitur **male sana** sororem:
"Anna soror, quae me suspensam **insomnia** terrent!
quis novus hic nostris successit sedibus hospes,
quem sese ore ferens, quam forti pectore et armis!"

quibuscum in fauces

saucius, saucia, saucium	wounded
alo, alere, alui, altum	I feed
carpo, carpere, carpsi, carptum	I wear away
haereo, haerere, haesivi, haesum	I am stuck to, cling to
vultus, vultus, m	face, but in plural, means eyes
posterus, postera, posterum	next
Phoebeus, Phoebea, Phoebeum	of Apollo
lustro, lustrare, lustravi, lustratum	I light up
Aurora, Aurorae, f	Aurora (goddess of the Dawn)
polus, poli, m	sky
male sana	in distress
insomnium, insomnii, n	dream, nightmare

46. Dido makes a sacrifice at the altar, to help her decide what to do as she falls deeper and deeper in love with Aeneas.

(Aeneid IV, lines 61-70)

ipsa, tenens dextra **pateram**, pulcherrima Dido
candentis vaccae media inter cornua fundit,
aut ante ora deum **pinguis spatiatur** ad aras,
instauratque diem donis, pecudumque reclusis
pectoribus inhians spirantia consulit **exta**.
heu **vatum** ignarae mentes! quid vota furentem,
quid **delubra iuvant**? **est** mollis flamma **medullas**
interea, et tacitum vivit sub pectore **volnus**.
uritur infelix Dido, totaque vagatur
urbe furens, qualis coniecta cerva sagitta.

quibuscum in fauces

patera, paterae, f	sacrificial bowl
pinguis, pinguis, pingue	rich
spatior, spatiari, spatiatus sum	I wander
instauro diem	I renew the day
exta, extorum, n pl	entrails
vates, vatis, m	priest
delubrum, delubri, n	shrine
iuvo, iuvare, iuvi, iutum	I am of use, benefit
est	eats away at
medulla, medullae, f	marrow
volnus = vulnus	

47. Queen Dido appears in front of the Carthaginian leaders and the Trojans, dressed for the royal hunt. Iulus and Aeneas march along in the procession.

(Aeneid IV, lines 133-142)

reginam **thalamo** cunctantem ad limina primi
Poenorum exspectant, **ostroque** insignis et auro
stat **sonipes** ac frena ferox spumantia mandit.
tandem progreditur magna stipante **caterva**
Sidoniam picto **chlamydem** circumdata **limbo**;
cui **pharetra** ex auro, crines nodantur in aurum,
aurea purpuream subnectit **fibula** vestem.
nec non et Phrygii comites et laetus Iulus
incedunt. ipse ante alios pulcherrimus omnis
infert se socium Aeneas atque agmina iungit.

quibuscum in fauces

thalamus, thalami, m	bedchamber
Poeni, Poenorum, m pl	Carthaginians
ostrum, ostri, n	purple
sonipes, sonipedis, m	horse
caterva, catervae, f	crowd
chlamys, chlamydis, f	cloak
limbus, limbi, m	border
pharetra, pharetrae, f	quiver
fibula, fibulae, f	brooch

48. *During a storm, Dido and Aeneas seek shelter in a cave, where the elements around them combine to encourage their lovemaking. After this, the real problems began.*

(Aeneid IV, lines 162-172)

et Tyrii comites passim et Troiana iuventus
Dardaniusque nepos Veneris diversa per agros
tecta metu **petiere**; ruunt de montibus amnes.
speluncam Dido dux et Troianus eandem
deveniunt. prima et **Tellus** et **pronuba Iuno**
dant signum; **fulsere** ignes et conscius aether
conubiis summoque **ululauunt** vertice Nymphae.
ille dies primus leti primusque malorum
causa fuit; neque enim specie famave movetur
nec iam furtivum Dido meditatur amorem:
coniugium vocat, hoc **praetexit** nomine culpam.

quibuscum in fauces

tectum, tecti, n	shelter
petiere = petiverunt	
Tellus, Telluris, f	Tellus, the earth goddess
pronuba Iuno	Juno the goddess of marriage
fulsere = fulserunt	
ululaunt = ululaverunt	
praetego, praetegere, praetexi, praetectum	I cover

49. Aeneas and his men sailed away from Carthage, when they saw the flames of Dido's funeral pyre. They remained unaware of the cause, as they journeyed through open seas towards a darkening storm.

(Aeneid V, lines 1-11)

interea medium Aeneas iam classe tenebat
certus iter fluctusque atros **Aquilone secabat**
moenia respiciens, quae iam infelicis **Elissae**
conlucent flammis. quae tantum accenderit ignem
causa latet; duri magno sed amore dolores
polluto, **notumque** furens quid femina possit,
triste per **augurium** Teucrorum pectora ducunt.
ut pelagus tenuere rates nec iam amplius ulla
occurrit tellus, maria undique et undique caelum,
olli caeruleus supra caput astitit imber
noctem **hiememque** ferens et **inhorruit** unda tenebris.

quibuscum in fauces

certus, certa, certum	fixed, determined
Aquilo, Aquilonis, m	the North Wind
seco, secare, secui, sectum	I cut through
Elissa, Elissae, f	Dido
conluceo, conlucere, conluxi	I shine, grow bright
notum, noti, n	knowledge
augurium, augurii, n	foreboding
olli = illi	
caeruleus, caerulea, caeruleum	dark-coloured
hiems, hiemis, f	storm
inhorresco, inhorrescere, inhorrui	I grow rough

50. Aeneas calls his men together and tells them it has been exactly one year since his father Anchises died. It is a day they should feel sad about but also proud.

(Aeneid V, lines 42-50)

postera cum primo stellas **Oriente fugarat**
clara dies, socios in **coetum** litore ab omni
advocat Aeneas **tumulique** ex **aggere** fatur:
"Dardanidae magni, genus alto a sanguine divum,
annuus exactis completur mensibus **orbis**,
ex quo reliquias divinique ossa parentis
condidimus terra maestasque sacravimus aras;
iamque dies, nisi fallor, adest, quem semper acerbum,
semper honoratum (sic di voluistis) habebo."

quibuscum in fauces

Oriens, Orientis, m — the East, sunrise
fugarat = fugaverat
coetus, coetus, m — meeting, assembly
tumulus, tumuli, m — hillock
agger, aggeris, m — mound
orbis, orbis, m — cycle
ex quo — since, from when
condo, condere, condidi, conditum — I bury

51. *In the boat race, as the crowd roar their encouragement, Cloanthus sees Mnestheus aproaching and prays to the gods to help him win.*

(Aeneid V, lines 227-238)

tum vero ingeminat clamor cunctique sequentem
instigant studiis, resonatque fragoribus aether.
hi proprium decus et **partum indignantur** honorem
ni teneant, vitamque volunt pro laude **pacisci**;
hos successus **alit**: possunt, quia posse videntur.
et **fors** aequatis cepissent praemia **rostris**,
ni palmas ponto tendens utrasque Cloanthus
fudissetque preces divosque in vota **vocasset**:
"di, quibus imperium est pelagi, quorum aequora curro,
vobis laetus ego hoc candentem in litore taurum
constituam ante aras voti **reus**, extaque salsos
proiciam in fluctus et vina liquentia fundam."

quibuscum in fauces

instigo, instigare, instigavi, instigatum	*I cheer on*
hi – refers to the people on Cloanthus' ship	
pario, parire, peperi, partum	*I win, acquire*
indignor, indignari, indignatus sum	*I consider unworthy*
paciscor, pacisci, pactus sum	*I bargain*
hos – refers to the people on Mnestheus' ship	
alo, alere, alui, altum	*I sustain*
fors	*perhaps*
rostrum, rostri, n	*beak of a ship*
vocasset = vocavisset	
constituo, constituere, constitui, constitutum	*I set up*
reus, rei, m	*someone who repays*

52. The ghost of his father Anchises appears to Aeneas and tells him that he must make a journey to Latium. First, however, Aeneas must visit the Underworld, to receive instructions about his journey: the Sibyl will help in his quest.

(Aeneid V, lines 730-740)

"gens dura atque aspera cultu
debellanda tibi Latio est. **Ditis** tamen ante
infernas accede domos et **Averna** per alta
congressus pete, nate, meos. non me impia namque
Tartara habent, tristes umbrae, sed **amoena** piorum
concilia Elysiumque **colo**. huc casta Sibylla
nigrarum multo pecudum te sanguine ducet.
tum genus omne tuum et quae dentur moenia disces.
iamque vale; torquet medios Nox umida cursus
et me saevus equis **Oriens** adflavit **anhelis**."
dixerat et tenuis fugit **ceu** fumus in auras.

quibuscum in fauces

Dis, Ditis, m	Dis, Pluto (god of the Underworld)
Avernus, Averna, Avernum	from Avernus (the Underworld0
congressus, congressus, m	meeting
amoenus, amoena, amoenum	happy, pleasant
concilium, concilii, n	gathering, meeting
colo, colere, colui, cultum	I inhabit
Oriens, Orientis, m	Dawn
anhelus, anhela, anhelum	panting
ceu	like

53. *After the helmsman Palinurus fell into the sea and was drowned, the fleet sailed on and eventually Aeneas himself took over at the rudder of his ship.*

(Aeneid V, lines 862-871)

currit iter tutum non **setius** aequore **classis**
promissisque patris Neptuni **interrita** fertur.
iamque adeo **scopulos** Sirenum advecta **subibat**,
difficilis quondam multorumque ossibus albos
(tum rauca adsiduo longe **sale** saxa sonabant),
cum pater amisso fluitantem errare **magistro**
sensit, et ipse ratem nocturnis rexit in undis
multa gemens casuque animum concussus amici:
"O nimium caelo et pelago confise sereno,
nudus in ignota, Palinure, iacebis harena."

quibuscum in fauces

setius	otherwise
classis, classis, f	fleet
interritus, interrita, interritum	unafraid
scopulus, scopuli, m	rock
subeo, subire, subii	I come up to
sal, salis, m	surge, salt
magister, magistri, m	steersman

54. Anchises reveals the shades of Julius Caesar and Augustus to Aeneas, as he shows him a glimpse of Romans who will be born in the future.

(Aeneid VI, lines 789-795)

> hic Caesar, et omnis Iuli
> progenies, magnum caeli ventura sub axem
> hic vir, hic est, tibi quem promitti saepius audis,
> Augustus Caesar, Divi genus, aurea condet
> saecula qui rursus **Latio**, regnata per **arva**
> Saturno quondam; **super** et **Garamantas** et **Indos**
> proferet imperium.

quibuscum in fauces

Latium, Latii, n	Latium (area around Rome)
arvum, arvi, n	land
super	in addition, moreover
Garamantes, Garamantum, m pl	Garamantes (an African tribe)
Indi, Indorum, m pl	Indians

Introduction to Cicero unseens

Cicero was without any possible doubt the most important of all Roman prose writers. He was an orator, lawyer, politician and philosopher, as well as being a writer of many published letters. In this collection of passages, you will find examples of his writing from across all areas of his activities.

Most students find Cicero difficult to translate, so don't be put off if this is the case. The main thing is always to find a starting point in a sentence, which is normally the main verb. Do this before you begin to attach any real meaning to the text in front of you and your chances of success will improve.

Cicero was a very vain man, who always enjoyed talking about his own importance to the Roman Republic. It is easy to criticise him for this, but we should also remember that most well-known Romans were by nature arrogant and full of themselves. They had to be, as self-promotion was the best way to get on in their world. Cicero had a right to his self-importance, perhaps, because he came from outside of Rome and had not been born into its highest echelons. He prided himself on being a *novus homo* – a new man - who had made it to the top of the Roman establishment.

In what follows, there are passages from his philosophical writings, speeches and letters. At the end, there are two passages included which were not written by Cicero himself: one is from his correspondent Caelius and the other is Seneca the Elder's account of the great man's death.

Even if you dislike Cicero and his windbag pomposity, you should realise that he was the foremost thinker and speaker of the Roman world. When the crucial time came, he stood by his principles and even died for them. His words continue to resonate in the modern world, perhaps more than those of any other Roman writer.

In order to gain a good idea of what Cicero achieved and how important he was, you should read the books *Imperium* and *Lustrum*, by Robert Harris. They will give you a deeper understanding of his life and work and if you are interested enough in Latin to be using this book, you should find them fascinating, without being at all difficult to read. Highly recommended.

55. In his treatise About Divination, Cicero mentions a dream he had once had, about seeing his brother on horseback near a river.

(de divinatione I.28)

saepe tibi meum narravi somnium; me, cum Asiae **pro consule** praeessem, vidisse in quiete, cum tu, equo **advectus** ad quandam magni fluminis ripam, **provectus** subito atque delapsus in flumen nusquam apparuisses, me contremuisse timore perterritum; tum te repente laetum **exstitisse** eodemque equo adversam ascendisse ripam, nosque inter nos esse complexos.

quibuscum in fauces

pro consule	as a proconsul
advehor, advehi, advectus sum	I ride towards
provehor, provehi, provectus sum	I ride forwards
exsisto, exsistere, exstiti	I step out

56. Cicero refers to events at the time of the battle of Numantia, when Quintus Pompey had made a treaty without the approval of the Senate. This was initially supported by the ex-consul Philus but later he attacked Pompey for showing too much self-interest.

(de re publica III.28)

quod in singulis, idem est in populis: nulla est tam stulta civitas, quae non iniuste imperare malit quam servire iuste. nec vero longius abibo: consul ego **quaesivi**, cum vos mihi essetis in consilio, de **Numantino foedere**. quis ignorabat Q. Pompeium fecisse **foedus**, eadem in causa esse Mancinum? alter vir optimus etiam **suasit rogationem** me ex senatus consulto ferente, alter **acerrime** se defendit.

quibuscum in fauces

quaero, quaerere, quaesivi, quaesitum	I pursue a policy
Numantinus, Numantina, Numantinum	of Numantia
foedus, foederis, n	treaty
suadeo rogationem	I support a bill
acriter	disgracefully

57. Cicero writes to his friend Atticus, stating the case of his philosophical work, On Old Age. He hopes that his discussion will enable the process of growing old to be undergone with fortitude.
NB – Atticus' name refers to Attica, the area around Athens.

(de senectute 1-2)

novi enim moderationem animi tui et **aequitatem**, teque non **cognomen** solum Athenis **deportasse**, sed humanitatem et prudentiam intellego. nunc autem visum est mihi de senectute aliquid ad te conscribere. hoc enim **onere**, quod mihi commune tecum est, aut iam **urgentis** aut certe adventantis senectutis et te et me etiam ipsum levari volo; etsi te quidem id **modice** ac sapienter, sicut omnia, et ferre et laturum esse **certo** scio.

quibuscum in fauces

aequitas, aequitatis, f	sense of well-being
cognomen, cognominis, n	name
deportasse = deportavisse	
deporto, deportare, deportavi, deportatum	I take from
onus, oneris, n	burden
urgeo, urgere, ursi	I press upon, approach
modice	calmly
certo	for certain

58. Cicero talks about the two possibilities of death, which should not worry somebody of advancing years. There are two choices: either it brings an end to the soul, or it allows its removal to a place of eternal life. Neither eventuality is to be feared.

(de senectute, 14)

quarta restat **causa**, quae maxime **angere** atque **sollicitam** habere nostram **aetatem** videtur, appropinquatio mortis, quae certe a senectute non potest esse longe. O miserum senem qui mortem contemnendam esse in tam longa aetate non viderit! quae aut plane neglegenda est, si omnino exstinguit **animum**, aut etiam optanda, si **aliquo** eum deducit, ubi sit futurus aeternus; atque tertium certe nihil inveniri potest.

quibuscum in fauces

causa, causae, f	argument
ango, angere, anxi, anctum	I cause pain
sollicitus, sollicita, sollicitum	disturbed
aetas, aetatis, f	age, age group
animus, animi, m	soul
aliquo	to some place

59. In his discussion, About Destiny, Cicero discusses the ideas behind the atomic theories of Democritus and Epicurus, where natural forces affect the movements of particles. He wonders if they should apply towards free-will, freedom of choice and the human spirit.

(de fato 23, with omissions)

hanc Epicurus **rationem** induxit ob eam rem, quod veritus est, ne, si semper atomus gravitate ferretur naturali ac necessaria, nihil liberum nobis esset, cum ita moveretur animus, ut atomorum motu **cogeretur**. Democritus, **auctor** atomorum, accipere maluit, necessitate omnia fieri cum enim concessissent motum nullum esse sine causa, non concederent omnia, quae fierent, fieri causis **antecedentibus**; **voluntatis** enim nostrae non esse causas externas et **antecedentes**.

quibuscum in fauces

ratio, rationis, f	theory
cogo, cogere, coegi, coactum	I drive
auctor, auctoris, m	inventor
antecedo, antecedere, antecessi, antecessum	I precede
voluntas, voluntatis, f	free will

60. In his philosophical treatise, On the Nature of the Gods, Cicero says that the entire debate about the existence of the gods cannot be based on knowledge, but that it is good for the soul and essential for keeping control of superstition.

(de natura deorum I.1, slightly adapted)

cum multae res in philosophia nequaquam satis adhuc explicatae sint, tum perdifficilis, Brute, quod tu minime ignoras, et perobscura quaestio est de natura deorum, quae et ad **cognitionem animi** pulcherrima est et ad moderandam **religionem** necessaria. de qua tam variae sint doctissimorum hominum tamque discrepantes **sententiae**, magno **argumento** esse debeat ea causa, **principium** philosophiae esse inscientiam.

quibuscum in fauces

cognitio, cognitionis, f	discovery
animus, animi, m	soul
religio, religionis, f	superstition
sententia, sententiae, f	opinion
argumentum, argumenti, n	proof
principium, principii, n	beginning

61. *Cicero asks Catiline why he should want to stay in Rome when only a small group of conspirators still continues to support him, and everyone knows about his disgraceful crimes and behaviour.*

(in Catilinam, I.VI)

quid est enim, Catilina, quod te iam in hac urbe delectare possit? in qua nemo est extra istam coniurationem perditorum hominum, qui te non metuat, nemo, qui non oderit. quae **nota** domesticae turpitudinis non **inusta** vitae tuae est? quod privatarum rerum **dedecus** non haeret in fama? quae libido ab oculis, quod facinus a manibus umquam tuis, quod flagitium a toto corpore afuit?

quibuscum in fauces

nota, notae, f   mark
iniuro, inurere, inussi, inustum   I burn into
deducus, deducoris, n   disgrace

62. *In defending Milo against the charge of killing Clodius, Cicero asks which of the two of them would have chosen the place of the attack.*

(pro Milone, XX)

videamus nunc (id quod caput est) locus ad insidias ille ipse, ubi congressi sunt, **utri** tandem fuerit aptior. id vero, iudices, etiam dubitandum et diutius cogitandum est? ante fundum Clodi edito adversari atque excelso loco, superiorem se fore **putarat** Milo, et ob eam rem eum locum ad pugnam potissimum elegerat? an in eo loco est potius exspectatus ab eo qui ipsius loci spe facere impetum **cogitarat**? res loquitur ipsa, iudices, quae semper **valet** plurimum.

quibuscum in fauces

uter, utra, utrum	which one of two
putarat = putaverat	
cogitarat = cogitaverat	
valeo, valere, valui, valitum	I prevail

63. Cicero sums up in his defence of the consul Murena. He hopes that the judges will vote for him to be acquitted, as it will bring benefit to the Republic and to the consul's home town, Lanuvium.

(pro Murena XC, slightly adapted and shortened)

iudices, conservate populi Romani beneficium, reddite rei publicae consulem, date generi et familiae, date etiam Lanuvio, **municipio** honestissimo, quod in hac tota **causa** frequens maestumque vidistis. quem ego vobis consul consulem, iudices, ita commendo ut cupidissimum oti, studiosissimum bonorum, acerrimum contra **seditionem**, fortissimum in bello, inimicissimum huic coniurationi quae nunc rem publicam labefactat futurum esse promittam.

quibuscum in fauces

municipium, municipii, n   town
causa, causae, f   case, courtcase
seditio, seditionis, f   rebellion

64. *In his prosecution of Verres, the corrupt governor of Sicily, Cicero says sarcastically that although Verres openly plundered the province, his defence rests on the fact that he also protected it during times of danger.*

(in Verrem, II.5.1)

nemini video dubium esse, iudices, **quin** apertissime C. Verres in Sicilia sacra profanaque omnia et privatim et publice **spoliarit**, versatusque sit sine ulla non modo **religione** verum etiam dissimulatione in omni genere **furandi** atque **praedandi**. sed quaedam mihi magnifica et praeclara eius defensio ostenditur; ita enim causa **constituitur**, provinciam Siciliam virtute istius et vigilantia singulari dubiis **formidolosisque** temporibus a fugitivis atque a belli periculis tutam esse servatam.

quibuscum in fauces

quin	that, but that
spolio, spoliare, spoliavi, spoliatum	I plunder
religio, religionis, f	religious scruple
furor, furari, furatus sum	I rob
praedor, praedari, praedatus sum	I take booty
constituo, constituere, constitui, constitutum	I set up, establish
formidolosus, formidolosa, formidolosum	terrifying

65. Cicero asks Hortensius if he should really defend Verres on the grounds that he was a general. He hopes he will not follow a practice of the former orator Mark Antony, who had once exposed his client's wounds at the end of a speech, to arouse the sympathy of the court.

(in Verrem, II.5.32)

hunc tu igitur **imperatorem** esse defendis, Hortensi? huius furta, rapinas, cupiditatem, crudelitatem, superbiam, scelus, audaciam rerum gestarum magnitudine atque **imperatoriis** laudibus **tegere** conaris? hic scilicet est **metuendum** ne ad exitum defensionis tuae vetus illa Antoniana dicendi **ratio** atque auctoritas proferatur, ne **excitetur** Verres, ne denudetur a pectore, ne **cicatrices** populus Romanus aspiciat, ex mulierum morsu vestigia libidinis atque **nequitiae**.

quibuscum in fauces

imperator, imperatoris, m	victorious general
imperatorius, imperatoria, imperatorium	suited to a general
tego, tegere, texi, tectum	I cover up
metuo, metuere, metui, metutum	I fear
ratio, rationis, f	practice, method
excito, excitare, excitavi, excitatum	I bring out
cicatrix, cicatricis, f	scar
nequitia, nequitiae, f	worthlessness

66. Cicero introduces the first Philippic by talking about why he had once left Rome and returned. After Caesar's assassination, he had decided to stay in Rome, because he was optimistic that the Senate's power was being returned to it and felt it was his duty to remain.

(Philippics I.1)

antequam de republica, **patres conscripti**, dicam ea, quae dicenda hoc tempore arbitror, exponam vobis breviter consilium et **profectionis** et **reversionis** meae. ego cum sperarem aliquando ad vestrum consilium auctoritatemque rem publicam esse revocatam, manendum mihi statuebam, quasi in **vigilia** quadam **consulari** ac **senatoria**.

quibuscum in fauces

patres conscripti senators (conscript fathers)
profectio, profectionis, f voyage (from Rome)
reversio, reversionis, f return (to Rome)
vigilia, vigiliae, f watch
consularis, consularis, consulare of an ex-consul
senatorius, senatoria, senatorium of a senator

67. Cicero talks about what happened at a meeting in the Temple of Tellus, two days after Caesar's murder. On this occasion, he had urged a policy of forgiveness, along the lines of that once used by the Athenians, after a period of tyranny was ended.

(Philippics I.1)

nec vero usquam discedebam nec a re publica deiciebam oculos ex eo die, quo in **aedem Telluris** convocati sumus. in quo templo, quantum in me fuit, **ieci** fundamenta pacis Atheniensiumque renovavi vetus exemplum; Graecum etiam **verbum** usurpavi, quo tum in **sedandis** discordiis **usa erat** civitas illa, atque omnem memoriam discordiarum oblivione sempiterna delendam censui.

quibuscum in fauces

aedes, aedis, f	temple
Tellus, Telluris, f	Tellus, an earth goddess
iacio, iacere, ieci, iactum	I cast
verbum, verbi, n	phrase
sedo, sedare, sedavi, sedatum	I settle, calm down
utor, uti, usus sum + ablative	I use

68. In the second Philippic, Cicero asks the audience to focus their attention on Antony's corrosive effect on the Roman world. His personal life is one thing, but the wider scale of his influence has been devastating to Rome.

(Philippics II.50)

accipite nunc, quaeso, non ea, quae ipse in se atque in domesticum dedecus impure et intemperanter, sed quae in nos fortunasque nostras, id est in universam rem publicam, impie ac **nefarie** fecerit. ab huius enim scelere omnium malorum **principium** natum reperietis.

quibuscum in fauces

accipio, accipere, accepi, acceptum	I pay attention to
nefarie	wickedly
principium, principii, n	beginning

69. Cicero continued to attack Antony in the third Philippic, referring to the disgrace and insolence shown towards the republic by the behaviour of people in his household.

(Philippics III.35)

nostis insolentiam Antoni, nostis amicos, nostis totam domum, libidinosis, petulantibus, impuris, impudicis, **aleatoribus**, ebriis **servire**, ea summa miseria est summo **dedecore** coniuncta. quodsi iam - quod di omen avertant! - fatum extremum rei publicae venit, quod gladiatores nobiles faciunt, ut honeste **decumbant**, faciamus nos principes orbis terrarum gentiumque omnium, ut cum dignitate potius cadamus quam cum ignominia **serviamus**.

quibuscum in fauces

nostis = novistis
aleator, aleatoris, m — gambler
servio, servire, servii, servitum — I am a slave
dedecus, dedecoris, n — disgrace, dishonour
decumbo, decumbere, decubui, decubitum — I lie down to die

70. Cicero talks about whether it was right to call Octavian Caesar a victorious general, after his defeat of Antony's army. The fact that Octavian was so young would lead him to think this title might not be appropriate, had it not been for his exceptional bravery and courage.

(Philippics XIV.28)

an vero quisquam **dubitabit** appellare **Caesarem imperatorem**? aetas eius certe ab hac sententia neminem deterrebit, quandoquidem virtute superavit aetatem. ac mihi semper eo maiora **beneficia** C. Caesaris visa sunt, **quo minus** erant ab aetate illa postulanda; cui cum imperium dabamus, eodem tempore etiam spem eius nominis **deferebamus**; quod cum est **consecutus**, **auctoritatem** decreti nostri rebus gestis suis comprobavit.

quibuscum in fauces

dubito, dubitare, dubitavi, dubitatum — I hesitate
Caesar, Caesaris, m — Octavian Caesar
imperator, imperatoris, m — victorious general
(a title conferred by the Senate)

beneficium, beneficii, n — good quality
quo minus — as... less...
defero, deferre, detuli, delatum — I take into account
consequor, consequi, consecutus sum — I obtain
auctoritas, auctoritatis, f — good sense

71. In defending Roscius, Cicero asks the presiding magistrate Marcus Fannius to act vigorously in punishing the crimes committed by those bringing the accusations. Otherwise, he says, there could be civil disturbance in the Forum.

(pro Roscio Amerino, XII)

petimus **abs** te, M. Fanni, a vobisque, iudices, ut quam **acerrime** maleficia vindicetis, ut quam fortissime hominibus audacissimis resistatis, ut hoc cogitetis, nisi in hac causa, qui vester animus sit, ostendetis, eo prorumpere hominum cupiditatem et scelus et audaciam, ut non modo clam, verum etiam hic in foro ante tribunal tuum, M. Fanni, ante pedes vestros, iudices, inter ipsa **subsellia caedes** futurae sint.

quibuscum in fauces

abs = ab
acriter harshly
subsellium, subsellii, n courtroom bench
caedes, caedis, f bloodshed

72. Cicero explains how a delegation of ambassadors from Ameria came to Chrysogonus with a petition, seeking to bring to Sulla's attention the appropriation of Sextus Roscius' land. Chrysogonus made every effort to stop the matter from reaching Sulla.

(pro Roscio Amerino, XXIV-XXV)

atque ipsum **decretum**, quaeso, cognoscite. **legati** in castra veniunt. intellegitur, iudices, id quod iam ante dixi, **imprudente** L. Sulla scelera haec et flagitia fieri. nam statim Chrysogonus et ipse ad eos accedit et homines nobilis **adlegat**, qui peterent, ne ad Sullam adirent, et omnia Chrysogonum, quae vellent, esse facturum pollicerentur. usque adeo autem ille **pertimuerat**, ut mori mallet, quam de his rebus Sullam doceri.

quibuscum in fauces

decretum, decreti, n	petition
legatus, legati, m	ambassador
imprudens, imprudens, imprudens	unaware
adlego, adlegare, adlegavi, adlegatum	I send (as an agent)
pertimesco, pertimescere, pertimui	I become very scared

73. Cicero defends the practice of defending clients. He argues that the justice system needs people to be put on trial, as long as they are not made a fool of, to allow them chance to prove their innocence in court.

(pro Roscio Amerino, LVI)

accusatores multos esse in civitate utile est, ut metu contineatur audacia; verum tamen hoc ita est utile, ut ne plane inludamur ab **accusatoribus**. innocens est **quispiam**, verum tamen, quamquam abest a culpa, suspicione tamen non caret qua re facile omnes **patimur** esse quam plurimos **accusatores**, quod innocens, si accusatus sit, **absolvi** potest, nocens, nisi accusatus fuerit, condemnari non potest; utilius est autem **absolvi** innocentem quam nocentem **causam** non **dicere**.

quibuscum in fauces

accusator, accusatoris, m — prosecutor, accuser
quispiam, quaepiam, quodpiam — anyone, someone
patior, pati, passus sum — I allow
absolvo, absolvere, absolvi, absolutum — I acquit
causam dicere — to answer a charge in court

74.   Cicero recalls a story when two sons were accused of parricide in Terracina, after their father's dead body was found in a room where they had been staying together. They were acquitted because they had been able to sleep soundly, without even locking the door.

(pro Roscio Amerino, LXIV- LCV)

non ita multis ante annis aiunt T. Caelium quendam Terracinensem, hominem non obscurum, cum cenatus **cubitum** in idem conclave cum duobus adulescentibus filiis isset, inventum esse mane **iugulatum**. cum neque servus quisquam reperiretur neque liber ad quem ea suspicio **pertineret**, nomina filiorum de parricidio **delata sunt**. tamen, cum planum iudicibus esset factum aperto **ostio** dormientis eos repertos esse, **iudicio** absoluti adulescentes et suspicione omni liberati sunt.

quibuscum in fauces

cubo, cubare, cubui, cubitum	I sleep
iugulo, iugulare, iugulavi, iugulatum	I strangle
pertineo, pertinere, pertinui	I am attached to
defero, deferre, detuli, delatum	I report
ostium, ostii, n	door
iudicium, iudicii, n	court

75. Cicero refers to the laws of proscription, which permitted the property of the victims to be sold off legally. He says that if Roscius was not proscribed or found among the enemies of the state, his property should not have been sold.

(pro Roscio Amerino, CXXVI)

scriptum enim ita dicunt esse: UT AUT EORUM BONA **VENEANT** QUI PROSCRIPTI SUNT; quo in numero Sex. Roscius non est: AUT EORUM QUI IN ADVERSARIORUM **PRAESIDIIS** OCCISI SUNT. dum **praesidia** ulla fuerunt, in Sullae **praesidiis** fuit; postea quam ab armis omnes recesserunt, in summo **otio** rediens a cena Romae occisus est. si lege, bona quoque lege **venisse fateor**. bona quo iure aut quo modo aut qua lege **venierint** quaero.

quibuscum in fauces

veneo, venire, venii, venitum	I go on sale, am sold
praesidium, praesidii, n	garrison, defence
otium, otii, n	peace-time
fateor, fateri, fassus sum	I admit

76. *In a letter to Atticus, Cicero talks about a meeting he has had with Hortensius and how he preferred his company to that of Antony, who was his colleague as an augur. Atticus had been recovering from an illness and Cicero wishes him well.*

(ad Atticum X.16)

CICERO ATTICO SAL.

sed, dum redeo, Hortensius venerat et ad me Terentiam salutatum deverterat. **sermone** erat usus **honorifico** erga me. iam eum, ut puto, videbo; misit enim **puerum** se ad me venire. hoc quidem melius quam conlega noster Antonius, cuius inter lictores lectica **mima** portatur.

tu quoniam **quartana** cares et novum morbum removisti sed etiam **gravedinem**, teque **vegetum** nobis in Graecia siste et litterarum aliquid interea.

quibuscum in fauces

sermo, sermonis, m	tone of conversation
honorificus, honorifica, honorificum	respectful
puer, pueri, m	slave
mima, mimae, f	actress
quartana, quartanae, f	a four-day fever
gravedo, gravedinis, f	head cold
vegetus, vegeta, vegetum	lively, well

77. Cicero writes to Varro about the imminently expected arrival of Caesar. He has been advised that the dictator would first come to land at Alsium, but thinks that Ostia would be more suitable for the purpose.

(ad familiares IX.6, slightly adapted)

Caninius noster me tuis verbis admonuit, ut scriberem ad te, si **quid** esset, quod putarem te scire oportere. est igitur adventus Caesaris scilicet in exspectatione, neque tu id ignoras. sed tamen, cum ille scripsisset, ut opinor, se in Alsium venturum, scripserunt ad eum sui, ne id faceret; multos ei molestos fore ipsumque multis; Ostiae videri commodius eum **exire** posse.

quibuscum in fauces

quid — anything
exeo, exire, exii, exitum — I disembark (from a ship)

78. Cicero writes to Brutus complaining in strong terms about having received such a short letter from him in such momentous times. He says that his own letters are always more substantial.

(Cicero ad Brutum, I.14)

CICERO BRUTO SAL.

breves litterae tuae - breves dico - immo nullae. tribusne **versiculis** his temporibus Brutus ad me? nihil scripsisses potius. et requiris meas! quis umquam ad te tuorum sine meis venit? quae autem epistula non **pondus** habuit? quae si ad te **perlatae** non sunt, ne **domesticas** quidem tuas **perlatas** arbitror. **Ciceroni** scribis te longiorem daturum epistulam. recte id quidem, sed haec quoque debuit esse plenior.

quibuscum in fauces

versiculus, versiculi, m — short line
pondus, ponderis, n — substance, weight
perfero, perferre, pertuli, perlatum — I deliver
domesticus, domestica, domesticum — domestic (means from a family member)

Cicero, Ciceronis, m — (refers to Cicero's son)

79. Caelius wrote this letter to Cicero in 50 BC. In it, he says he fears the increasing danger to the Republic, created by the mutual hostility and distrust of Caesar and Pompey: civil war is gradually becoming a reality.

(ad familiares VIII.14)

de **summa** re publica saepe tibi scripsi me in annum pacem non videre et, **quo** propius ea **contentio** quam fieri necesse est accedit, **eo** clarius id periculum apparet. **propositum** hoc est, de quo qui rerum **potiuntur** sunt **dimicaturi**, quod Cn. Pompeius constituit non pati C. Caesarem consulem aliter fieri nisi exercitum et provincias tradiderit, Caesari autem persuasum est se **salvum** esse non posse si ab exercitu recesserit.

quibuscum in fauces

summa, summae, f — chief matter
quo... eo... — as... so...
contentio, contentionis, f — dispute
propositum, propositi, n — main point
potior, potiri, potitus sum (+ gen) — I am in control of
dimico, dimicare, dimicavi, dimicatum — I struggle
salvus, salva, salvum — safe

80. The Elder Seneca describes how Cicero met his death, after being pursued by the agents of his enemies. He was being carried in a litter near his villa by the sea, when he gave in to his fate with stoic fortitude.

(Seneca the Elder, SUASORIAE VI.17)

taedium tandem eum et fugae et vitae cepit regressusque ad superiorem villam, quae paulo plus mille passibus a mari abest, "moriar," inquit, "in patria saepe servata." satis constat servos fortiter fideliterque paratos fuisse ad **dimicandum**; ipsum deponi **lecticam** et quietos pati quod fors iniqua cogeret iussisse. prominenti ex **lectica** praebentique immotam cervicem caput **praecisum est**.

quibuscum in fauces

taedium, taedii, n	disgust
dimico, dimicare, dimicavi, dimicatum	I struggle
lectica, lecticae, f	litter, bier (on which Cicero was being carried)
praecido, praecidere, praecidi, praecisum	I cut off

ALSO AVAILABLE - IMPERIUM LATIN COURSE

The Imperium Latin course has been written for the twenty-first century; unique, highly resourced and written to make fullest use of modern technology. Its texts follow the life of the Emperor Hadrian, from his early childhood to his later years, as he became the most powerful man in the Roman world.

Imperium was released for general use in 2013, after a trialling period of six years. It consists of three coursebooks, a Grammar and Syntax Guide and the Imperium Latin Unseens collection for advanced users. All of these texts can be ordered through Amazon but are also available as pdf files in either one of our two Site Support Packs, which can be bought by schools. The coursebooks are also available as free of charge downloadable pdf files, from the TES Resources website.

For further details, see www.imperiumlatin.com

PUZZLE BOOKS FROM J-PROGS

These collections are aimed at those who want to have some fun with the languages they know and love. All books feature solutions at the back, for those who get stuck.

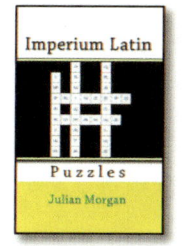

Imperium Latin Puzzles was written for those who follow the Imperium Latin Course but could certainly be used by students of other courses. It contains 60 puzzles and features sudokus, word searches, Latin to English crosswords and English to Latin ones.

Easy Latin Puzzles was written after compiling three lists of words commonly used in a variety of Latin courses. It makes very limited use of word endings and includes a variety of challenges, including sudokus, word searches, Latin to English crosswords and English to Latin ones. The book features the full word lists at the back.

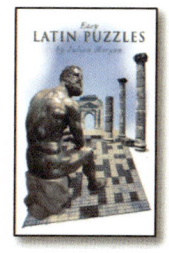

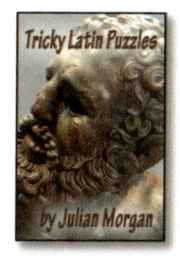

Tricky Latin Puzzles was written for students learning Latin today or for those to whom the good old days beckon. These 50 crossword puzzles, sudokus, wordsearches and other brainteasers should bring plenty of fun. It is aimed at those who have studied the language for two or three years at least.

Easy Greek Puzzles was assembled from two short lists of words commonly used in a variety of courses. It uses all five cases of noun, adjective and pronoun systems, as well as the active indicative verb endings from the present, imperfect, aorist and future tenses. As such, it is suitable for those who have studied the language for one year or longer. The 50 puzzles include sudokus, wordsearches, Greek to English crosswords and English to Greek ones.

Tricky Greek Puzzles was written for those whose command of ancient Greek may allow them to enjoy its challenges - not for the faint-hearted. It includes 50 crosswords, sudokus, wordsearches and other brainteasers and is aimed at those who have studied the language for two or three years at least.

For details on how to get your copies, see www.j-progs.com

ABOUT THE AUTHOR

Julian Morgan served as a teacher and a Head of Classics for many years in the UK, before taking up a post in 2007 at the European School of Karlsruhe in Germany. Julian has devoted his entire career to finding new, original ways of teaching Latin and Greek.

Julian has written many educational software titles and books in the last 25 years, publishing a range of these under the banner of his business, J-PROGS. He is well known in Classics teaching circles for his teacher training activities, not least in directing courses for the CIRCE Project, which has been part of the EU's Comenius programme since 2003. He has served twice as a Council member of the Joint Association of Classical Teachers and has also been a long-standing member on the Computing Applications Committee of the American Classical League.

The Imperium Latin course was first published in 2013 and is being adopted in a growing number of schools, where its digital materials are helping to promote good learning. It consists of three coursebooks, a Grammar and Syntax Guide, the Imperium Word Tools App, and a wide range of other electronic support material. All of this content has been designed to make best of of today's technology in the classroom, while adhering to traditional values of Classics teaching.

He can often be found walking his dogs in the Great Wold Valley of North Yorkshire, where he lives.

You can find out more on Julian's Author Page:
amazon.com/author/julianmorgan